His. Not Mine.

RESTING IN GOD'S CARE

STEPHEN APPLE

The Simple Guide to Peace & Purpose in Life

DEDICATION

This writing is dedicated to my wonderful wife, Patricia. Without her love and patient encouragement I would have never completed the work. It is also dedicated to my brothers and sisters in Jesus Christ who labor throughout the world to carry the love and peace of God to the hopeless and despairing. Labor in His strength and compassion. The day of His redemption is near.

CONTENTS

A Simple Prayer

"You Lord have made the universe and all creatures great and small. You have poured the seas and raised the mountains. You have set the stars in the infinite vastness of the universe and given miraculous life to the countless creatures on earth, the creatures in the sea, and the birds that fly in the air. And You alone understand all the intricacies of the creation that You have created. Lord, you have made mankind in Your image that we might have the capacity to understand how great and glorious You are.

You understand completely both the physical and spiritual parts of who we are. You see all our thoughts before any of them come forth. You have known us when we were in the womb and before our first breath was breathed. And in Your mercy You have saved us from judgement of our sins. We will not perish when we receive Your salvation which, in love, You have given us. Oh Lord, how You love mankind! How You love us. How You love me, Lord. When I consider Who You are, and what You have done, and the love You have shown me in Your Son Jesus Christ, I am drawn to give my life back to You."

Amen.

Introduction

In Jeremiah 10:23, the prophet acknowledges to God that we are completely unable to plan our own lives. They were created for God's plans and purposes. So why are we anxious about our own plans in life? Is it not better to simply believe … to simply trust … simply love God? He will guide you in all that is life. This is the key to life as a child of God. Its radical truth stands unmovable against all the so called wisdom of man. Its message describes a journey leading to treasure beyond all imagination.

Understanding its foundation brings peace and serenity as constant companions. The storms of life fade as they are demoted to insignificance. The journey begins with the uttering of a simple statement acknowledging this truth … "My life is His. Not Mine." Saying it awakens the journey, an itinerary beyond all imagination. A tiny seed, buried deep within, begins its miracle; its birth forged in secret. Tomorrow's season witnesses its tiny form breaking the hardened ground and reaching toward the light. Heaven welcomes a child. Beginning today, God will take your hand and patiently and lovingly show you the wonders of His care. Now is the time to discard those worries. You will not be needing them any longer. Rest in His hands. Shelter in His love. You are greatly treasured by the Creator of all things. Now, your life is His. Finally, you can rest.

Some of the following chapters were crafted from joy experienced. Others birthed from the seeds of heartache. Many were penned in perplexity … wondering what God was doing. All were redeemed in hope and concluded in agreement that God is good, and that He loves us greatly. The journey arrives at one treasure … Peace with God. All else in life is secondary.

CHAPTER 1
"HIS LIFE. NOT MINE."

"I know, Lord, that our lives are not our own. We are not able to plan our own course."
Jeremiah 10:23 NLT

The rumble of the truck idling outside my window in the Israeli inner city use to disrupt my imagination as I wrote. The smells of the auto exhaust rise uninvited through my open window from the crowded streets below. Their lanes conversing in a strange language of honking horns; betraying the anxieties chasing them forward. In earlier years it rudely interrupted the quiet listening for God's whispers. Yet now it's rather a central part of the story He's gently painted upon my thoughts. In the Tel Aviv metroplex, I'm surrounded by 2.4 million people who, though they speak a different language, have the same concerns in life as I do. They have questions, and the same need for God's love and forgiveness. They don't yet know exactly what they're seeking. But they know that, whatever it is, peace is in there somewhere. And that's the reason the Lord has placed my wife and I, and countless others, in the land for varying allotments of time. His peace is needed. We have His peace. It's a match made in Heaven.

Much like us, you also have been called and thoughtfully placed to bring hope to the despairing and light into the darkness. As a messenger on earth, God has placed you. In His love He has saved you and forgiven your former wickedness. Even your current mistakes are covered by His atoning sacrifice. You are now His; tenderly cared for by Him.

In the days fashioned for your life, He intricately and patiently unfolds the mystery of your calling. Day to day pours forth knowledge. Nightly His Spirit explores your thoughts; reshaping and organizing those deemed unfinished. In wisdom He orders your steps, and whispers to your heart which path to take. He inspires upon your wonderings the words and wisdom needed for each divine encounter He has purposed to bring your way.

You were created to be His child. He has called you to be a messenger of His mercy. He has placed you in a strange land through which you sojourn as a foreigner whose heart is set on home. Your own testimony of His mercy and forgiveness attests to His compassion. Now your story can bring peace to the hopeless and lead them to a loving home, eternal in the heavens. Entrusted to you is your Heavenly Father's offer of salvation to all who will hear His voice.

This is the central purpose of your existence now. Whatever form your calling may take, it is always shaped from the clay of God's love. This is your true calling; to love God, and to love others. All His commandments arrive in unanimous agreement at this destination.

"Beloved, let us love one another: for love is of God; and every one that loves is born of God, and knows God."

1 John 4:7 KJV

You are His treasure; created that He could care for you, lead you, protect and provide for you. He loves you as His very own child. He greatly desires you, and He greatly desires to use you for purposes far more noble than mere existence. You can rest in assurance that He will be with you each step, every day, in every thought; guiding every decision. This is the inheritance of a child of God.

But so often we don't realize, or we forget, why we are here, and we stumble blindly through life trying to design our own plans and goals. In doing so we miss the amazing life and purpose God has prepared for us. A breathtaking journey awaits those who hear His whispers and answer His invitation.

Life is not intended to be stumbled through, trying one thing after another in an endless search for purpose and fulfillment. God has a specific purpose for each of us. And in His wisdom, He has carefully placed us in the right places at the perfect times to be used for lofty tasks far above our understanding. We could never comprehend, let alone plan, the things that have been purposed for us in the mind of God. Life is far more complex than the limited scenes viewed through human eyes.

It has a physical component, and it has a spiritual dimension. Only God can guide you safely through life. It is far too intricate; it is too unpredictable to be successfully navigated by human understanding alone. The enemies of your life are much stronger and knowledgeable than you. Only God is all powerful, and only He can protect you from the forces that would rise against you. He alone is all wise, and He alone knows where to place you today to keep you from catastrophe tomorrow.

In Psalm 139:16 the writer reflects on God's plan for life saying,

"You saw me before I was born. Every day of my life was recorded in your book. Every moment was laid out before a single day had passed." NLT

God brought forth a plan for all of your days before any of them existed. And if you knew the plan that He has fashioned for you, your best-imagined efforts to plan life would look impoverished in comparison.

Even when you take great care to design your own plans for life, those plans are destined to fail. Does that seem like a radical statement? I agree. It is, in fact, radical. But it's also true. Jeremiah 10:23 calls out through time to warn us,

"We are unable to plan our own course." NLT

It does not say that we sometimes will fail in our planning. Nor does it say that, only if we try really hard, can we succeed in planning our own course in life. No, it concludes that all our attempts to plan our own lives will end in failure. Sure, there are fleeting moments when you think you have succeeded, but the passage of time and events reveal your lack of forethought once again. Then you attempt to adapt and adjust your plan, and you try again, only to fail again. Your hope, being placed in yourself, is flawed at the foundation.

The reality is when you hope only in yourself, you are alone and in danger among obstacles and enemies you cannot possibly imagine. But, as each year passes from life, you rekindle your resolve to plan smarter, think about things more carefully, and be stronger. If only you knew all the factors involved, you say. If only this situation had not arisen at this time or that. Yet in reality, the problem is not in the circumstances you face or the situations that changed. The problems are that you do not know what the future holds, and that you cannot defeat the enemies that will come against you.

But the world expects you to be strong. The world entices you to believe that you will eventually find the right revelation of wisdom to make your life right. After all, the stories painted by Hollywood on the screens extol the virtues of mankind and how the human spirit will always prevail.

They tell you how wise you are, and how strong you can become, and how things will eventually work out for you through shear human resolve. Only rarely is God invoked in their story. But, of course, the reality is that Hollywood is only fiction; something produced in the imagination of a person who only wishes the narrative were true. The actor, himself a person like you with problems of his own, simply recites the lines the script writer has given them in order to dress fiction as reality.

But real life is the opposite. In reality, you will only find fulfillment and happiness when you give your life to the Creator who made you. Only He can bring you contentment and purpose in life. The peace you seek is only to be found in Him.

But, while the Scriptures make it clear that you cannot plan your own way, the Bible is equally clear that God has the perfect plan for your life.

Consider the peaceful assurance given in Jeremiah 29:11,

"For I know the plans I have for you, says the Lord. They are plans for good and not for disaster, to give you a future and a hope." NLT

Taken together with Jeremiah 10:23, these passages speak of an amazing journey that can be yours when you take the courage to trust God in life. And He has promised to be with you always; never leaving you or forsaking you. He will always be there to keep you and to protect you. It really does make sense, after all. He is your Creator, and He created you to be His beloved child. Your innermost being is inseparably interwoven with the need for Him in your life. Nothing else can fill the place in you which God has created for Himself.

In Him is the contentment and purpose you seek in life. In Him is all you need in life. So how do you receive this happiness and peace that He offers? Simply acknowledge that you are unable to plan your own way, and ask instead for Him to guide you in life.

As stated above, when we trust in ourselves, we let ourselves down. God, however, will never let you down. So why not trust Him? Many would say that they know they should, but they just can't get comfortable with not knowing "how" things will work out. The stumbling block is the word, "how". We all want to know "how" things will work? But in the faith God is calling you to, you will not always see what He is doing in your life or how He will fix things as He guides you.

It's far more important to know "Who" will take care of you and "Who" will meet the situations that come against you. When you realize that the Creator of all things is with you always ... When you understand that He is all powerful ... And when you realize how much you mean to Him ... Then, all that matters is that He is with you; and that He is directing your steps. Leave the how, when and where to Him. All you need to know is Who will be with you. With God guiding you, everything will turn out well.

The author of the Book of Hebrews states, "Faith is the evidence of things not seen." So it follows that, if you need to see exactly what is happening as you go through life, you are not yet comfortable with living and walking by faith. Now perhaps you have always thought that living by faith is only for radical believers. Nothing could be further from the truth. Living by trusting in God is for all believers. It's the way God designed life to be lived.

Yes, living in faith is upside down from the ways of the world. But in reality it's the world that is upside down from the righteous ways of God. Our lives have been designed for communion with God; on a daily and continual basis. When we yield our lives to Him, we experience the unimaginable journey He has for us. We see the indescribable colors and landscapes of the spiritual side of our existence that are infinitely better than anything our imaginations could have painted. And as the journey will be beyond description, the rewards are likewise beyond compare.

But the decision to go forth on the faith journey requires a commitment, and that decision is yours alone to make. Your commitment must be made with resolve, for it is an everlasting commitment that has a beginning but no end. In Mark 8:34-35 Jesus said,

" ... *Whoever desires to come after me, let him deny himself, and take up his cross, and follow me. For whoever desires to save his life will lose it, but whoever loses his life for my sake and the gospel's will save it*" *NKJV*

Are you prepared to set forth on the journey? Do you have the desire and courage to set your own plans for life behind you and to set before you the daily desire to walk in God's care? Notice the first step forward is to deny yourself. What does that mean? Simply put your desire to walk with God before any other desire you may have in life. It's a struggle between you and yourself. And though the struggle may at first thought seem evenly matched, upon taking your first steps forward, God will strengthen you, and He will stand with you. He will give you the wisdom and resolve you will need in order to prevail. The key is to realize that it is only with Him that you can truly succeed in life.

As you can see, turning over everything to the Lord requires humbling yourself. You are admitting that your understanding is limited. You are acknowledging that your strength is not enough to meet the events that come against you. And humbling yourself is a difficult thing to do. The world and all our environment teaches people to be proud. But God says the proud will be brought low, and the humble will be exalted.

A decision must be made in the heart of the believer. You must consider, once and for all, who you are in life, and who you will serve. Will you, out of fear for what the world will think of you, try to blend in with the ways of the world? Or will you decide to simply stay on the sidelines and not take a stand for the world or for God? Or will you walk the fence trying to be both a citizen of the world and a child of God? Or will you take your stand for Jesus Christ and decide that your life belongs to God.

When you try to "blend in" you are hiding who you are. That means you are taking the light God has given you and hiding it from view. If that light is hidden it does no good to those around you. They continue to walk in darkness and despair and hopelessness because you have covered over your light. And, if you have covered over the light God has given you, then what happens to the purpose of your life? It has been nullified by your lack of courage.

As said above, too many times believers choose to hide who they are. But it's more than hiding who you are; it's hiding who He is from those who desperately need to know Him. If your life is completely His, then you are His light. He's not going to hide your light. He's going to put you on a lampstand where your light can be noticed and give light to those in the darkness.

Likewise, when you decide to stay on the sidelines, you are again hiding who you are and not bringing God's love to those around you as God has purposed for your life. You are not taking a stand for Jesus Christ in your life before those who need to see your testimony the most. Consider what Jesus said in Matthew 10:32-33 ...

"Everyone who acknowledges me publicly here on earth, I will also acknowledge before my Father in Heaven. But everyone who denies me here on earth, I will also deny before my Father in Heaven." NLT

You see, in reality, there is no neutral position. You either belong to Christ or you belong to the world. By not taking your stand for Christ, you are taking a stand for the world instead.

In the same way, when you try to live your life as a citizen of the world and a child of God, those around you will see that you are not the same person on Monday as you are on Sunday. In other words, they will see the hypocrisy in your life as you speak of lofty spiritual truths on some occasions, but are fluent in the ways of the world in others. By not having consistency and steadfastness in your beliefs, your testimony and calling in life is compromised. And you will not be effective in the purpose that God has designed for your life.

No, you must decide who you are and who you will serve. There is no avoidance of the decision. Everyone must take a stand. You will stand for Christ, or you will stand for the world. And that decision is yours alone to make.

Now, if you're still with us and reading this, I'm thinking you have made your decision, whether just now or long ago, to take your stand for Jesus Christ. So let's talk about going forward. Let's talk about living life as a child of God.

We've seen that God has a plan for each of us. And we know God's plan includes a calling. So each of us have a calling. Let's start there. How do we answer the calling that God has for us? It's common, in your joy as a child of God, to get excited about serving Him and to begin planning what you will be doing for Him and His kingdom. You start making your own plans and setting your own goals for that ministry. Recognize where this is going?

It's easy to consider all the abilities you believe you can bring to your calling, and to imagine all the experience you can bring to bear on the work that God has for you. In reality, however, out of all the abilities that you could offer the Lord, the only one He really needs from you is simply your "avail-ability". Are you available for God to use? In His plan? Are you available?

The key to the answer is humility. As we said earlier, God's wisdom is far above your own. He has known from the beginning of time what you would need to be fruitful in the ministry He purposed for your life. And He has equipped you with the proper gifts and talents to accomplish that calling.

So, you see, there is no room for personal glory to be taken. All that is done, and all that is accomplished, is from Him alone. He is the One who is present with you each and every step you take. And if He is the one directing each step; and if He is the One bringing His power to bear on each problem; then how has any experience of your own become important in your calling? Acknowledging that all glory from any accomplishment in life belongs, not to you, but to God alone is a natural conclusion to reach when your life is His and not your own.

It's a simple story, really. God created you. He created you in His image, and He has a plan for your life. He simply wants to use you as the person He has created you to be. He has designed into your personality all the unique traits and abilities He needs you to have to accomplish the mission to which He is calling you.

Like light, all you have to do is shine. Light just has to show up, and darkness loses. It's that simple. Just let the light radiate out of your life.

Look at what Jesus said in Matthew 5:14-16 …

"You are the light of the world. A city that is set upon a hill cannot be hidden. Nor do they light a lamp and put it under a basket, but on a lampstand, and it gives light unto all who are in the house. Let your light so shine before men, that they may see your good works and glorify your Father in Heaven." NKJV

Notice again that you are already a light to the world. All you have to do is shine and not try to hide the fact that you belong to God. He has put His Spirit within you. But, again, it's possible for you to hide the light that is within you. If that were not so, He would not have said *"Let your light shine …"*.

You have the choice to hide His light in your life, or to let His light shine out from you to others. If you are a light, you are His light. If your life is His, then you are there for His purposes. Therefore, shine where He has placed you. Your life is His ... Not Yours.

You were not created to be your own. You were created to be a child of God. You were created to be guided by Him and to be used by Him for things far higher than the meager plans you imagine for yourself. And the plan that God has for your life is the one that is uniquely designed to not only bring His purposes to pass, but to also bring you the most happiness, peace and fulfillment in life. You will be the happiest you could possibly be when God is at the center of your life and your life is in His hands alone.

You will never be content in life outside of His plan for you. But in surrender to Him, all things are yours. It's time to face the failures of your own plans, and the frailty of your own strength, and the limitations of your own wisdom. It's time to consider the reality of your existence as a child of God who was created by Him for amazing things. It's time to yield your life to Him completely and change direction in life. It's time to give everything to Him, holding nothing back, and say,

"From now on, my life is His. Not Mine."

CHAPTER 2
"HIS PLANS. NOT MINE."

"For I know the plans I have for you, says the Lord. They are plans for good and not for disaster, to give you a future and a hope."
Jeremiah 29:11 NLT

It's inappropriately early in the morning in Tel Aviv. Only a couple of people sit at the quaint little coffee shop tables around me. I always wake up so slowly. I'm not sure how my shoes knew how to get here. My small computer screen softly illuminates the small wooden table and the left side of my coffee cup positioned reassuringly close to my right hand. The city is largely still asleep, and the absolute darkness of the night sky is only slightly bothered by the scattered small lights which define the boundaries of the establishment. Against the darkness which surrounds me, it's impossible for my eyes to be drawn to anything other than my empty screen and the missing words which should be on it. They're probably playfully hiding somewhere behind the keys; daring me to find them. And they're clever. Caffeine will be necessary.

My heart is instructed that, even in the meager illumination which the computer offers, one's eyes are always drawn to the light. The Creator has wisely commanded the light to stand out in victory against the darkness, as if proclaiming the end of the story from the beginning. Light will be victorious. The day approaches.

As I think about the previous chapter I am set back because of its proclamation that we are absolutely unable to plan our own course. Yet I am comforted by the assurance of the verse above, that God has designed the perfect plan for each of His children.

As I write these words I am reminded of God's faithfulness in this very thing in my own life. I am, at this moment, sitting in a strange land half way around the world from the place where I lived most of my life. I would have never imagined coming here. I had plans of my own in those days, before taking wings and flying away to the unknown.

Upon arriving, so long ago, everything was strange and different to me. The whole experience was like watching a movie in a foreign language which I did not then understand. And though I now speak, awkwardly at times, the native Hebrew language of the Israelis, it was a long road. I remember thinking how strange it was to be learning Hebrew. After all, I was born and raised in Texas. You could make the case that I had never really learned English.

And yet now, after all these years, I am content; happier than I ever could have imagined. I have lost my life in this place. I have found myself in the place God imagined for me as He penned the pages of my life. Deep inside I sense this has been my purpose all along; to go to this people and proclaim His love to their despairing and hopeless. And though He called me here, He could not have chosen a more clueless individual.

It is by His mercy and patience that I now sit, surrounded by this surreal experience, amazed at His wisdom, care and faithfulness. As in a movie, life spins around me. And I, as an uncast actor in the story, attempt to fit in. I am as one who wandered aimlessly onto the set and nobody noticed.

My daily prayer remains that I would somehow contribute to the story which God Himself is producing. And yet I know that He has planned a small part for me somewhere in His story. He has known from the beginning of time the role I would play in His plan, and He reveals daily to me what is to be said; what is to be done.

It is not important that I understand His purposes or His methods. It is only important that I know that this story is

His, and that He is the writer, producer, director, and casting agent. As long as the story unfolds in agreement with His will, all will turn out wonderfully well. I just need to follow the Director; to go where He says, and say what He desires.

Consider something for a moment. When God imagines a plan, it's a flawless plan. All the details have been carefully considered, and any potential problems have been taken into account and answered in His perfect wisdom. This comforts me for two reasons. First, that God has taken the time and effort to think about me personally; out of all the people who inhabit our humble abode. Then, second, that He has not only designed the plan for me as one that will accomplish His purposes and bring glory to Him, but He has also designed it in such a way as to bring me the greatest happiness and fulfillment in life.

He didn't have to do that last part. He is God. He could have just said, "This is the way it's going to be. Deal with it." But, He was concerned about my happiness. That speaks volumes to me about who He is and how much I mean to Him. It seems that everything that He has done has been done to draw me to Him.

Imagine the promise of Jeremiah 29:11 being superimposed on your own life. What would it feel like to know that God Himself has carefully thought out all the days of your life? What excitement would your thoughts sense in knowing that He has meticulously crafted a plan to bring both purpose and happiness to your life?

Now briefly consider all your own, inadequate, plans that you have tried to force into submission through the years. It's liberating to know that struggle need not continue. You can rest in the plans that God has for your life knowing that they are perfectly designed for you. Think of the effort you have put into trying to carefully plan your own way. Recall all the tense deliberations about which paths you could take. Remember the fear of making the wrong decision and the "analysis paralysis" you found yourself in when unsure of which way to go.

As Jeremiah 29:11 confirms, you never really needed to go through all that. You could have simply rested and trusted God. He has the perfect plan for your life already. Simply trust in Him, and you'll be okay. In fact, God will lead you in the absolute best path for your life every day. This promise of continuous peace in life is confirmed as well in Isaiah 26:3,

"You will keep him in perfect peace whose mind is stayed on You, because he trusts in You." NKJV

As you can see, God places great value on His children trusting in Him and being assured of His love. And it's natural for Him to do that. What father would not want his children to feel secure in his love? No loving father wants his children to continuously live in fear and uncertainty; doubting whether he wants them or not. You are a child of the perfect, all powerful Heavenly Father. You are His child, and He wants the best for you.

He wants you to have peace and assurance in His love and care. He wants your relationship with Him to be one of enjoyment and love and blessing. Again, simply rest in His love and care. It takes all the stress from life and replaces it with a certain assurance that, behind the scenes, the Lord is causing everything around you to work out for the good. And it's all because you are His child.

Now, does all this talk about child-like faith sound a little simplistic to you? Does the thought of letting go and trusting God alone scare you? If it does, it really only comes down to one of two reasons.

First, it may be that you're unfamiliar with the concept of trusting God for the important decisions in life and your everyday care. Or, second, it may be that you understand you need to trust God, but you're a little uncertain about how much responsibility He wants you to take for life, and how much responsibility He wants you to yield to Him.

Okay, then ask yourself a simple question. In each specific aspect of life, which decisions is He better qualified than you to handle? The answer is obvious. God is God. His wisdom is perfect. It really is that simple. His understanding is higher than your understanding as the heavens are above the earth. You're His child, and you need His hands to hold you up. You need His wisdom and care to guide you. And that's the reality, isn't it? You are just a child. Compared to your Heavenly Father, we are children in our understanding. But the beauty is that you are His child, and you are greatly treasured by Him.

You may even acknowledge that your life belongs to God, but the way you rely on your own plans shows a disconnect between what you say and how you live. At the heart of not giving Him all your cares is simple fear.

As we said earlier, people are afraid they might misunderstand what their responsibility is in all of this. Some are even afraid that God might allow them to fail terribly because they are not trying hard enough or because they are duly paying for past sins. Still others simply don't want to yield to God's control because they're afraid He might not give them what they want for themselves in life.

But in reality, God wants you to cast ALL your cares on Him. He cares for you and wants to continually bless you in ways you simply are incapable of imagining. Your past sins have been lovingly atoned for by His Son, Jesus Christ. And in Him you stand not guilty before a righteous and holy God. It's not your righteousness, or the lack of it rather, that He sees. Instead He considers the righteousness of His Son that has enveloped your life.

As He said of the blemish-free Passover lamb in Exodus 12, when He sees the blood of the chosen sacrifice covering your life, He will "pass over" you in judgement. He is glorified when you trust in Him and place your life in His hands. Your life is His. You are His to send in life. This is how heaven works as well. His messengers, the angels, are directed by Him as they are dispatched on their missions. God is preparing you for everlasting life in His kingdom.

Let's look at some of the undeniable facts around the issues in an attempt to drag our reluctant flesh across the "faith finish line". The first fact is that only God knows the future. You don't. He knows where the traps and pitfalls of life will be along the road, and He can direct your steps around them.

Next, He will lead you to the green pastures and beside the still waters. You may remember the pleasures of times when you were in those green pastures and alongside those refreshing, cool streams of water. But you have no way of knowing how to get back to them. The Good Shepherd will lead you to them, daily, to keep you fed, rested and refreshed.

Then, the Good Shepherd will protect you, watch over you and keep you from harm. Just stay close to the Good Shepherd, and all will be well. Has He not demonstrated how much He loves you? Look at the journey He made to the cross to rescue you from harm and to give you everlasting life that you might be with Him forever.

Finally, God is all powerful. Being convinced of His love, we can also be certain that no one and nothing can stop Him from watching over us, protecting us and showering us with His blessings each and every day as He desires. Nobody can prevent Him. And nobody can take you out of His hands.

And the life He has prepared for you is far better than anything you could desire for yourself. In fact, there have been many who thought they had achieved their dreams only to see their plans turn to tragedy. God will steer you around those "false dreams" and lead you to true riches, blessings and peace in life. Don't settle for the false treasures born out of your own imagination. Your desires can deceive you and cause you to waste your life following after things that are not true treasures at all.

In our mission work in Israel I routinely see homeless people who travel around from the streets to the alleyways. They laboriously carry with them plastic grocery bags filled with various discarded items they've found on the streets and in trash cans. They jealousy guard these possessions from would be thieves and treat them as their "treasures" and symbols of status. When we approach them to help them with real treasures, they are at first suspicious of our intentions. But after we provide them with a warm blanket or a new coat for the winter, they quickly throw out the old things to make room for the new.

That's the way it is with our plans and dreams. Once we understand the things that God has for us, we quickly discard the false "treasures" to make room for the true riches. Don't settle for your own plans in life. They are not true treasures. God wants to bless you with real riches, eternal and enduring treasures. He wants to give you things that are designed specifically to bless you and make you happy. Throw out the old. Let God bring in the new. Let Him surround you and envelop you with true, eternal and enduring treasures such as your mind has never imagined.

The best case scenario in your own plan is a distant second place to what God wants to give you. And the worst case is that your own plans will lead to catastrophe; all because you did not know what would happen later. But God knows the future, and He is watching out for your safety and welfare. Life is too short and too precious to squander. Entrust your life to the Creator, and watch the wonderful things He will do.

Now, what happens when you make the decision to trade your plans for God's plan? Will you suddenly be able to see all the things that He has purposed for you and called you to? The answer is no. Again, it's not important what you know; it's important Who you know. You will find yourself in the battle and seeing things one day at a time. In battles there are setbacks and there are strategic setups. Some of the things you view as a step backward are really the times for grabbing a solid foundation so that you can strongly spring forward.

And things are not always as they appear to human understanding. In the middle of the journey, when victory cannot yet be seen, events may seem all random. Things are happening all around you, but none of them seem even remotely connected to the answers to prayer you seek. In these moments, it's tempting to think that God is too busy to hear your requests, or that you've done too much wrong to "win" His favor. Maybe you fear that He has abandoned you. If you believe these fears, then you're simply mistaken. The problem is that you do not always recognize His working in your life. And that's because His ways are not like yours. Remember how He says it in Isaiah 55:8-9,

"For My thoughts are not your thoughts, Nor are your ways My ways, says the Lord. For as the heavens are higher than the earth, so are My ways higher than your ways, and My thoughts than your thoughts." NKJV

So, it follows that you will not always see what He is doing in your life as He is guiding you through the problems you face. The fact is your wisdom is limited. His wisdom is perfect and infinite.

There are still other factors that hinder your ability to plan your own life. There is your consideration of who you really are. Often you see your life only in terms of its physical existence. But the truth is you're a much more sophisticated creation. You were created in the image of God. But what does that mean? Does that mean that somehow God looks like man? Because, after all, our physical body has a general type of appearance and characteristics which we classify as human. No, that's not what being created in God's image means.

The Scriptures teach that God does not have a physical body as we do, but that God is spirit. Remember John Chapter 4:24? Jesus states,

"God is spirit, and those who worship Him must worship in spirit and in truth." NASB

So then, if we are created in the image of God, we have a spirit. God is eternal spirit. And we, being created in His image, are designed by Him to also have an eternal spirit. In other words, we were designed to live forever. But the first verses of Genesis 6 states that man is "also flesh". So, even though we were created in the image of God (Spirit), we also have a body of flesh (Physical). And, in our fleshly wanderings from God, our sins have separated us from Him and the everlasting life we were designed for.

In God's Word, He has stated that He must judge sin. He also states that the punishment He must give for sin is death. And God's Word is sure, so sin cannot simply be ignored. Sin has consequence, and the penalty for sin must be paid.

In God's plan to save the world from sin, God provided salvation through the atoning death of His Son, Jesus Christ. God Himself, in the person of Jesus Christ, took our sins on his own sinless body on the cross. The innocent died for the guilty; so that the penalty for sin would be paid. But because He had no sin of His own, death could not hold Him, and He was raised from the dead. And all who believe on Him as Lord and believe that God has raised Him from the dead and call on His name will be saved and restored to the everlasting life in Heaven that they were designed for.

Now the reason I covered these basics of our faith here is to show you that wisdom for your physical, fleshly existence alone, is not enough to account for your total existence. You are also spirit. And there is a spiritual realm of our existence which must also be accounted for.

God's wisdom and plans for your life spans both your physical existence and your spiritual existence. He sees each action, but He also sees each thought and motive of your heart. When He cares for you, in His perfect wisdom, He cares for both the physical and spiritual aspects of your life.

Most people focus on their physical lives because, that's what they see and consider to be the most important aspect of their life. In reality, nothing could be further from the truth. It's the spirit that can live forever. The flesh is but a temporary dwelling which will soon decay away.

So you can see that, in our so-called human wisdom, we place the most importance on the least important things. In fact, there are many such areas of life in which we consider ourselves to be wise but are not.

Since we are limited in our understanding of our own true existence and are surrounded by the false wisdom of the world, we can see our need for God's perfect wisdom in life.

God is the Creator of all things, so He understands all things perfectly. And His wisdom is outside of the boundaries and limitations of time. His wisdom is perfect now, and it always has been perfect, and it will be perfect in the future. On the other hand, our so-called wisdom can change as we learn new knowledge. Some would say that man is evolving and getting wiser, but I present that the opposite, in fact, is true. The further that man distances himself from the Creator Who formed him, the more foolish man becomes. Separated from his Creator, man is in fact devolving; he's slowly perishing.

Who is the better to lead you through life? A human "expert" in the world's "wisdom"? Or God? The world's wisdom has been proven wrong repeatedly throughout history; even on critical global issues. The most successful "life consultants" have dubious records at best. And there are as many opinions about life management as there are so-called "life experts".

When your own physical life, and your eternal spiritual welfare, are on the line, only God's wisdom will do. And every day, your physical life and spiritual welfare hang in the balance. Do you trust your own understanding and knowledge to guide you through life? Let me ask you a question. Have you made mistakes in your physical life? Big mistakes? Of course you have. Then why would you trust yourself in matters of your eternal destiny and everlasting life? Doing so is simply pride, and Scriptures confirm abundantly that the proud will fall. Scriptures speak of the days when those of the world will profess themselves to be wise, but in so doing become as fools. Undoubtedly, we are living in those very days. May we be safe from their grasp and, rather, locked in God's love.

Isn't it strange how completely opposite the false wisdom of man is from the true wisdom of God? In the world of sin, pride is spoken of as a good thing. But in God's Word, pride is a severe sin and a destroyer of those who wear it. As God's Word warns us, the proud will fall, but the humble will be exalted.

But wait, you say, "Doesn't God help those who help themselves?". No. In fact, that urban myth of human "wisdom" is not in Scripture at all. The Biblical answer, quite the opposite of human reasoning, is rather that God helps those who cannot help themselves and admit it. And if you are reading this and you do not know Jesus Christ as Lord, then your misunderstanding will be eternally fatal unless you cry out to Him and ask Him for His salvation in your life while there is still breath to do so.

When it comes to matters of successfully navigating life and matters of eternity, trusting in your own knowledge, determination and strength only leads to hell. The enemies of God that would destroy your life are many and mighty. They are much stronger and much smarter than you. In the spiritual realm, without the protection and guiding of God, you easily fall for deceptions designed to rob you of everlasting life. The enemies of God would have you believe that the agenda you have for your own life is simply to represent your own interests. In reality, your fleshly interests intersect tragically with the plans of the evil one who would deprive you of eternal life. To be saved and have everlasting life in God's kingdom, it is essential to trust God alone. Only in His Son, Jesus Christ, is everlasting life, joy and true peace.

If you already believe in the Son of God, then great peace is yours. Realize that God wants to do His will, His plan, in your life. And rest in His love as He guides your steps. His wisdom is perfect yesterday, today and tomorrow. It is forever perfect. Perfect wisdom does not change. It does not need to. It is complete. God is all knowing. His wisdom will not change tomorrow when some so called "new knowledge" appears, because He knows all things … past, present and future … and He has known them all from the beginning of time. He is the Creator of all things, and His understanding is infinite. He is the only One you want guiding you through life. Only in Him is eternal safety and everlasting life in His glorious kingdom.

It's important to see yourself, every day, as His child. Then you can rest in your relationship to God and not be consumed with fear and uncertainty continually. Now, like any little child, you can still wander off on your own and get into trouble from time to time. But, God, as your wise Heavenly Father, will lovingly chastise you, forgive you and then continue patiently teaching you because you are His child. Even if you stumble, God will pick you up, dust you off, bind up your bruises and set you back on the right path.

You don't need to fear judgment because Christ has taken your sins on Himself. You are now in the family of God. Patiently raising a child is what a reasonable human parent does. How much more patient and loving is your Heavenly Father? He will always be there with you, and He will always hear your prayers and cries for help.

Now you offer, "But I don't see God answering my prayers. I realize that I'm certainly not perfect. I have sinned and, even though I want to serve God, I still fail plenty. Is God still with me? If He's still with me, why can't I see His plan?"

It's common for people to not recognize God's hand moving in the little things of life from day to day. But it's easy to see His fingerprints all over your life in the rear view mirror. Be patient. The Lord of Hosts never slumbers or sleeps. His eye is on the sparrow, and rest assured He is watching over you. His plan and purposes will become evident over time.

Imagine, for a moment, a large table in a large room. On the table is a 50,000 piece puzzle. You know the kind I mean ... with the really small pieces that all look similar. Most of the time, puzzles like this come in boxes that have a picture of what the assembled puzzle should look like. But God's puzzles don't reveal the finished product until it has all come together. In that way, you will know that it is

God who is putting the puzzle together and not you yourself. In the end the glory will undeniably be the Lord's.

For your part, all you see are occasional, seemingly random pieces that have connected together. For days and weeks, and maybe months, the small connections of pieces continues and forms only scattered, unrecognizable islands of joined pieces. But no real picture emerges. Then the connections themselves start joining with other islands and give you more information. Finally an image starts to emerge in your mind, and you begin to see the plan that God had purposed all along. Be patient. God's plan is perfect, and His timing is perfect. Just rest in Him, and He will bring about His purposes in your life in due time.

He has heard your prayers. He has seen your worries. He sees each frustration build and each fear collide with your peace. He has watched each tear fall from your eyes. And even when you fear that He has left you, He is still beside you watching over you. Remember beloved child of God, He has promised to never leave you or forsake you. You belong to Him. You can rest from anxiety. Set your heart on His Plans ... not your own.

CHAPTER 3
"FOR HIS REASONS. NOT MINE."

"And we know that all things work together for good to those who love God, to those who are called according to His purpose."

Romans 8:28 NKJV

It's another early morning at my favorite coffee shop. There's something peaceful about watching the sky go from darkness through endless shades of gold and blue in the march of the morning. It's a gentle, polite alarm clock of sorts; not like the rude one beside my bed. Like a long, stretching yawn, my fingers slowly awaken as they hunt the proper letters on the cold keyboard. That's the easy part. Finding the words will be more challenging.

As the waitress rounds the corner behind me, I hear the unmistakable sound of a small coffee spoon hitting the cobblestone floor. Out of reflex, I get up and retrieve it for her. She looks somewhat astonished; though pleasantly so. I feel somewhat out of place. It seems I am not only from a foreign land, but also from a foreign time. Though I'm older now, the customs of my youth have stayed stubbornly with me. My reflexes have betrayed my age. As I contemplate the seemingly insignificant event, my mind slowly awakens, at first through a fog, to remember my purpose at the impatiently waiting keyboard of my computer.

It seems to me, that since God has a wonderful purpose for your life, it follows that there are good reasons for the things he allows. The things He brings your way, or leads you to, are the building blocks for the plan He has for your life. There's times when life takes an unexpected turn. And, while sometimes it's a pleasant surprise, many times the changes leave us asking why. You were just getting somewhat comfortable with where you were, and now everything has changed.

The change has caught you by surprise, and you begin wondering why God would let something like this happen to you. At first you look for ways to stop the change and paddle back to the safety of the familiar shore. But the change just seems to become irresistibly stronger, and hope for returning to the comfort of the usual routine begins to fade.

Rather than trying to navigate life against the currents of change, why not look with eager expectancy for the new chapter that God is carrying you into? Why not enjoy the journey and explore your new surroundings, looking for clues that He has hidden for you to discover? You know His character. You understand how much He loves you. You must realize how, in every aspect of your life, He seeks to bless you, to use you, and to bless others through you.

As we saw in the previous chapter, God has given us a purpose in life. Your life is not some random collection of events. Everything that happens to you happens for a reason. But God does not always reveal those reasons to us at the time the events unfold. Sometimes we see His reasons much later. Some may not be revealed until we are overjoyed in His presence. The important thing to remember is that God has His reasons for the things He allows in your life.

Yes, changes will come, but have the right perspective when they do. At first a baby prefers to scoot around on the floor on all fours rather than going onto the more difficult, and slower, first steps of walking. But after the pages of the previous chapter in life have turned, the new possibilities are seen, and the joy of increased mobility brings a mischievous grin.

Some changes in life are immediately apparent and joyfully accepted. Others seem contrary to our expectancy and require patient prayer and submission to God to accept. Seeing that God must have allowed the change, you begin to wonder why. What could God be doing in your life? Imagining no answer, you ask Him. And you wait for an answer, but all you hear is silence. And yet, deep inside, you already know the answer. God is leading you into the unknown ... again.

Once again, He is asking you to trust Him. And, as the author of the Letter to the Hebrews states, "Faith is the evidence of things not seen." In other words, if you need to see the answers before you allow God to direct your life, then you're not walking in faith.

How out of place I would be if I were to demand of God the reasons for what He is doing in my life. As the Scripture in Isaiah 45:9 asks,

"Does the clay say to the potter, 'What are you making?'"
NIV

If you think about it, the main motivation for wanting to know another's reason for doing something is to evaluate whether or not you approve of such logic. But how can mere man evaluate the thoughts of God?

Your life is interwoven into the very fabric of all creation. You are unable to comprehend the reasons why God places you where He does. You certainly cannot imagine how your presence in that place might ultimately affect all who journey across your path.

But the infinite wisdom of God understands the ultimate effect of a single fallen leaf upon the entire forest in which it dwells. He traces the shadow of the tiniest bird across the face of a tumultuous ocean. He instructs the clouds where to cast their shade and knows the number of the raindrops that will fall during your lifetime. He orders the journeys of the winds and feeds every living creature. Such is the intricate reasoning of the mind of God. How can His thoughts be known by man, much less evaluated?

The Merriam-Webster Dictionary defines "reason" as, "a fact, condition, or situation that makes it proper or appropriate to do something, feel something, etc."

Think about that for a moment. There are three factors that can make actions proper and right. The factors can be a fact that requires a certain response, a condition exists in which only certain actions are effective, or a situation that must be answered in a certain way to avoid calamity.

Only God sees all the facts surrounding your life. Your view is limited, and while you may spend a lot of time looking at the facts, you still only see the facts from a human perspective. You also are limited to the facts that do not deceive you and to facts that are not in your future. You don't see the facts that are not immediately before you.

Facts beyond your view or knowledge escape you. So then, how can you make a good decision about how to proceed?

Then, only God has a complete view and knowledge of the constantly changing conditions surrounding your life. As the blue skies can quickly give way to the approaching storm, the conditions in life can change from serene to dangerous. Unexpected conditions arise that derail your best plans in life.

But, again, God knows all things that are and all things that will be. He understands the conditions and the factors that gave them rise. He is the Creator, and He sees all creation with perfect understanding. When He examines the conditions that are present and has reason to respond in a certain way, His logic and reasoning are perfect.

Finally, God not only knows every storm that is developing and every fact that is a factor in your life, but He also sees each situation. Situations can change when the world around you changes, but they can also change with the words and actions of other people. Your own life can be greatly affected by the words and actions of others. Some actions, such as received words of kindness, are welcome. But other acts of people, such as violence, gossip, lies or contention, are unwelcome. God is the One who searches the hearts of man. He knows what is in each mind, and He hears the words of each utterance before they are brought forth. He can position you safely away from harm and shield you from the hostile attacks that come your way.

He takes all these factors into consideration when deciding on the best course of action to keep you safe. At the same time, He is also considering how to direct you around the dangers and bring you onward to the place He needs you to be.

Whatever God decides to do in your life, it's not only something that will bring Him glory and show His righteousness. It's also the thing that is needed to protect His beloved child. Your happiness and welfare is very important to God.

When you see that God has allowed something in life that was contrary to your own reasoning, rejoice! Because He has saved you from hardship you would have experienced by making the wrong decision. There's other times when God brings something into your life that you didn't ask for. And you're confused at what God plans for you to do with it. But He brought it to you because He knew that, down the road, it would be a great blessing to you. Again, rejoice! You don't have to have it all figured out, because you're a child of God. He's just caring for you because He loves you so much. You can rest.

He also loves you enough to say "no" to the things that might hurt you. You might greatly desire something, but

God knows it would bring you heartache. So, in His love, He sometimes says "No". And remember, "No" is also an answer to prayer. As I look back in life, I am very thankful for the times when God's answer to my prayer was "No". From where I stand today, I can now see that many times He saved me from terrible mistakes by refusing to give me what I asked for.

He also notes your response when your wayward petitions are denied, and He endures the lack of trust on your part. But He also smiles as you mature, and look back and thank Him for not answering your requests in the ways you wanted. In that day, you will understand that He had something much better for you all along.

Be patient as you wait for His answers. He has heard your prayers, and, at the perfect time, He will bring the perfect answer. Whether for a moment or a season, He is not ignoring you nor has He forgotten you, but He is patiently working in your life to form the image of His Son in you. The imprinting of His heart upon yours is a labor of love, and He is patiently shaping the clay to produce a vessel of honor. The creative hands of the Creator will produce their inevitable fruit in the seasons ahead. It frees your heart to know that not only do you not need to worry, but in fact He has made it easier for you by commanding you not to.

God not only sees the bigger picture around you today. He also sees the future. He is aware of not only the dangers presently surrounding you, but those in the days to come as well. Since you cannot see such times yet, you go about your daily life oblivious to where the road will turn treacherous. And God will sometimes try to "persuade" you to change your plans. But things unseen do not seem to be the pressing issues to human understanding. So God will, at times, use adversity to lead you to a place you would have otherwise never gone on your own.

That's the way it was with Joseph in his story in the Book of Genesis. It's the perfect example of how God's reasons are beyond the comprehension of the human mind. Let's spend some time on this intriguing Biblical story and let its words encourage us and stretch our faith.

 Joseph was one of twelve sons of the patriarch Jacob (who is called Israel). Joseph was not liked by his brothers. In fact, they resented him so much they sold him as a slave into nearby Egypt. Betrayed by his own brothers, Joseph found himself alone in a strange place far away from home. His brothers even lied to their father about Joseph and gave him the impression that Joseph had been killed by a wild animal. In doing so, they locked out all hope from Israel's mind that Joseph would ever return.

So, not only was Joseph alone, but he was relegated to a memory ... someone who no longer mattered in his family's day to day lives. Yet even in his painful situation, Joseph acknowledged the sovereign hand of God in His life. In his heart, Joseph knew that none of these events had taken God by surprise. He understood that God had seen all these things transpire before any of their days had dawned. He knew that the Omni-Present Creator was, even now, watching over Him and directing His steps in the strange place where he had found himself.

Before long Joseph, being a man who walked with integrity before God, had caught the attention of the captain of the guard who reported to Pharaoh, King of Egypt. As a servant of the captain of the guard, Joseph had certain daily responsibilities that he had to take care of. The captain of the guard noticed that everything that Joseph did was somehow blessed. Everything Joseph touched turned out good. In fact, the more responsibility the man gave Joseph, the more the man was blessed. Eventually he gave Joseph responsibility for everything he owned. And God blessed the man on Joseph's account.

But the man's wife soon became attracted to Joseph and tried to lure him to have an affair with her. Time after time Joseph resisted her. Finally, she became angry with Joseph's rejection of her invitation, and she accused him of trying to attack her sexually. It was a lie, but the damage had been done. The master of the house had Joseph thrown into the prison used for the King's prisoners. All that Joseph had worked for had been destroyed. He was now back to where he had started from.

Joseph could have become bitter against God, but he trusted that God had reasons for allowing this to happen. He knew that, even though the events looked like a setback, that God works in wonderful ways and would take what the enemy meant for evil and turn it into good. That setback would turn out to be a springboard that would launch Joseph forward into a blessing that he never could have imagined.

After a while in the prison, two new prisoners showed up. They were the baker and the cup bearer for the King himself. In his usual way of showing others encouragement and hospitality, Joseph would check on the other prisoners and try to cheer them up. He would talk about the God he served and, even in the dark prison, Joseph would proclaim His goodness.

One day, Joseph noticed the two new prisoners appeared very sad and troubled. Upon asking them why they were troubled, Joseph was told about a dream that each of the men had seen during the night. The two dreams were vivid, and each told a story of great importance, but that was all each man knew of their respective dream. They didn't understand what their dreams meant. Joseph boldly told the men that interpretations belong to God, and that He would provide the interpretations for their dreams.

As the men listened intently to Joseph, he prayerfully told the men the interpretations that God had given him. The details of the dreams and their interpretations, given in Genesis Chapter 40, came to pass a few days later. As the dreams had revealed, one of the prisoners was restored to the service of the King, and the other prisoner was executed. Joseph had asked of the acquitted man that he would remember him and mention him when the man returned to serving the King.

But, after the release of the prisoner, Joseph was again forgotten. That is, Joseph was forgotten by everyone except God. God never forgot Joseph. There were reasons in the mind of God why He had kept Joseph in the prison. And those reasons would only be known two full years later.

At that time, the King of Egypt himself had a dream that troubled him. It was a cryptic dream, vivid in its details and mysterious in its meaning. The King was greatly troubled, and the dream weighed heavily on his mind. He called for all the wise men of Egypt and told them the dream, but none of them could give the King its interpretation.

Then the chief butler, who had previously been released from the prison two years earlier, told the King about the young Hebrew man in the prison who could interpret dreams. Joseph was called to the presence of the King, and the pages of Joseph's life story began to turn to the next chapter.

God gave Joseph the interpretation of Pharaoh's dream, and the King was so impressed by the young man's wisdom that he made him second in command in all of Egypt. The King's dream had revealed there would be seven more years of good crops, followed by seven years of severe famine in the land. He put Joseph in charge of storing up the food in the good years before the great famine hit the land, and told the people to do whatever Joseph said. Then, as time went by, the King began to see the interpretation of his dream come to pass exactly as Joseph had said.

Here's the key to this story. God had reasons for allowing Joseph to be sold into slavery in Egypt. He had reasons for letting Joseph be falsely accused by the captain of the guard's wife. God needed Joseph to be in that dark and dreary prison at exactly that time that the two officials of Pharaoh would arrive as prisoners. Because Joseph was there, he was able to interpret the prisoners' dreams. And because he was able to interpret the prisoners' dreams the King's butler was able to tell the King about Joseph when the King himself had a dream.

God had foreseen this chain of events before they ever occurred, and He made a plan to use Joseph to gain favor from the King and to be placed by the King over all the food distribution at a time of great famine. If Joseph had not received that position of authority, much of Egypt, and even Joseph's own family in Canaan, would have perished in the famine. And if his family would have perished in the famine, the Messiah could have never come from the lineage of Jacob (Israel) and his son, Judah as prophesied. If the Messiah had never come as prophesied, then you and I would still be in our sins with no hope of Heaven. But, thank God, His Messiah has come and given salvation to all who believe on Him, among whom we stand.

Even in Joseph's wildest, most deliberate calculations and planning, he would have never foreseen these events. But Joseph knew that God cared for him and that God had reasons that were infinitely higher than his own understanding.

Indeed, here was a young man whom we would all do well to emulate. His example of trusting God, without demanding an understanding of God's reasons, is the Biblical model of faith we all should aspire to. It is only in trusting God that we will be content and truly able to rest in life. Trusting God plants a peace deep inside that no event of the world could ever take away.

The story of Joseph is a wonderful example of the verse in Romans 8:28 that is quoted at the first of this chapter. God can take anything, even the bad things, and turn them into the best things that ever happened to us. These were not insignificant troubles that came upon Joseph, but no situation is so severe that God cannot turn it upside down and bring great blessings from it.

Now, in all that happened, it would be easy to think that God was the one who brought these trials upon Joseph. But the Bible doesn't say that. God was able to take what the enemy meant to destroy Joseph and his family, and turn it into good.

As we said above, these events were meant to destroy Joseph's family so the Messiah could not come through them as the prophesies had foretold. The enemy of God had sought to defeat the prophecies that would bring the Messiah.

The devil attempted this because of his hatred of God. He hates God because God's angels cast him out of heaven following his attempt to promote himself as God. Since he could not fight against the all-powerful Creator, the devil turned his attention to destroying mankind. He knew that God loved mankind, and that God had created them in His own image to be His children. By preventing the Messiah from coming, all mankind would have perished in their sin with no hope of everlasting life.

But God used what the devil meant for evil and turned the situation into a great blessing instead. As a result, all those who believe in Jesus the Messiah and the work He did on the Cross will be saved and live forever. Their sins have been atoned for though the Messiah. As Romans 8:28 had said, God caused all the events that came Joseph's way to work together for the good. And, as a child of God, this is the guaranteed protection and care that is yours as well.

Notice that God can use adversity to bring you to a place that you would not have gone on your own. It's easy to get comfortable where you are and stop moving forward in the work that God has for you. Sometimes we wish to stop and rest at the pleasant place which we have found. Looking down on the valley below, we have no desire to leave our mountain top and traverse the trials of the lowlands. Nor do we consider that on the other side of the valley is a far more beautiful mountain experience that God desires to lead us to. So, sometimes, God has to bring adversity into life to move you on to a place you would have never gone on your own. He knows what's best for you, and He knows what's blessed for you!

He wants to keep you in His service. He has invested a great deal in raising you and training you for the work of His Kingdom. Plus, He is raising you and tutoring you for your own maturity and benefit in life. You can retire from work in the world, but don't ever retire from work in God's Kingdom. That work is what your life is all about. You can retire from your job, but don't ever retire from your calling. Don't ever retire from life.

His calling for you is your true purpose on earth! And your life in Him is a continuing journey. He desires to lead you and use you as long as there is breath in you. Your story is written by Him in His book, and the number of its pages is known to Him alone. He is the Author and Finisher of your story, and it is His alone to write its beautiful ending.

Psalm 139:16 says it this way,

"Your eyes saw my substance, being yet unformed. And in Your book they all were written, the days fashioned for me, when as yet there were none of them." NKJV

Now any book has chapters in which the main character goes through different situations. There are the beautiful mountain tops where all is well. And there are the valleys below where the trials break up all the hardened ground. But it's in the trials of the valleys where the growth occurs and God's faithfulness is learned.

There are different settings where the character finds himself. Sometimes he is brought to the new setting because of his own wanderings. At other times, circumstances beyond his control carry him away to a strange new place and a new situation. In your story as well, chapters are written through which you wander in a journey of discovery.

When God turns the page, and you find yourself in a new chapter, don't be afraid. It's just your loving Heavenly Father at work planning your impact in His harvest and laying the foundation for blessings He desires to bestow upon you. The change has not surprised Him. In fact, its clay has been formed by the Potter and lovingly decorated by Him to be a blessing that awaits you.

He has already planned the good that He will do through you and the blessings He has reserved for you in the new chapter. Walk unafraid into that chapter. The Creator of the universe is beside you and has promised to never leave you or forsake you. He is holding your hand. He is not finished with you. His desire is to use you all of your days. As long as there is breath in your body, God will use you to do wonderful things. He will do greater things through you in the next chapter of life.

As you can see from the story of Joseph, God's reasons are infinitely beyond our understanding and may go far beyond our current circumstances and even our approaching seasons. How beautiful are the ways of the Lord. How wonderful and infinite is His understanding. We are incapable of knowing and understanding His reasons.

As the Scripture confirms in Isaiah 40:13,

"Who can fathom the Spirit of the Lord, or instruct the Lord as His counselor?" NIV

It is indeed impossible to discover His reasoning, but it is enough to know His love. If you cannot understand His reasons, then you are certainly unqualified to approve of them. Walk in child-like manner into the comforting light of living and trusting in Him. From this day on resolve that you will rest in the knowledge that He has perfect reasons for the things He brings and the things He allows in your life. Say to Him, "Father, from now on I rest in the fact that Your reasoning is much higher than my own. Let my thoughts and steps be directed every day by Your Holy Spirit for Your Reasons ... Not Mine."

CHAPTER 4
"HIS RIGHTEOUSNESS. NOT MINE."

"Jesus answered and said to them, 'This is the work of God, that you believe in Him whom He sent."
John 6:29 NKJV

My feet are on auto-pilot as they stumble along the early morning walk of a couple of miles to the quaint little all night coffee shop. In fact, as I study that last sentence it seems somewhat like a self-fulfilling prophecy. The caffeine predicts the early awakening and subsequent journey to the place where the cycle repeats.

There are hundreds of little coffee shops in Tel Aviv, but the closer ones have not yet opened their eyes and put on their smiles. I walk toward my morning cup as a beagle on the trail of a rabbit. I should not be so chained to a small container of liquid, but, alas, here I am. I tell myself I can quit at any time. Which, I guess, is somewhat true. After all, I quit coffee three times just last year. I take consolation that the studies of the substance have not yet concluded if it is good for me or bad. So I guess I'm in a holding pattern for now.

As I sit at the small table, cup within comforting reach, the darkened skies slowly, almost reluctantly, awaken. It's easier to consider the subject of this chapter in the dream-like state of the early morning before the horns that roam the streets begin to call out to each other.

Being in Israel, I'm reminded of the mindset of the Jewish people toward the subject of righteousness; specifically the twenty percent or so in Israel who are religious Jews. The struggle to keep the law of the Bible is somewhat alluring; lending an air of humility and righteousness to those so inclined. Seekers? Certainly. Finders? Not so much. In fact, the very thing they attempt, in their desperate effort to find peace, embitters many as those efforts to subdue the guilt fail. Indeed, as the Scripture stated in Galatians 3:24,

"Therefore the Law was our tutor to bring us to Christ, that we might be justified by faith." NKJV

In other words, the Law was given to show that we could never really keep all the law completely. It was given to lead us Christ; to make us give up, and ask God for mercy.

The Law was given to reveal the ineffectiveness of our own resolve to live righteously. Its commands conclude all under sin that God might have mercy on all. Then, having secured our salvation Himself, He would be the source of our salvation and not ourselves. Therefore, the complete story of righteousness ends with the statement that to Him alone belongs all the glory. He alone is our salvation. As the Scripture itself confirms,

"Salvation is from the Lord."
Jonah 2:9 NASB

As I consider the deceptive lure of righteousness through works, I am struck at the similarities between the religious Jews and Christians. Could it be that many Christians as well feel constant guilt at not having done all the things they feel they should? Could it be they also feel that God is disappointed in them because they, too, fail from time to time? Let's wander down that path a bit and think this through.

The Jews, in their desire to present themselves righteous before God, endeavor in exhaustion to keep all the commands the Bible lists in the Law. They also try to adhere to the myriad volumes of commands their rabbis have added through the centuries. When they inevitably fail they sense that their efforts are somehow lacking, and that they must now try harder. And let's be honest with ourselves, we never really feel that we have succeeded in keeping all the Law. Any sense of accomplishment is fleeting and, before long we begin to question whether the nuances of the commands were properly adhered to.

In this environment, bitterness and doubt can easily surround the heart. In the mind the question arises, "Why has God made it so impossibly hard to keep His commands?" A certain resentment sets in, and any joy parachutes from the heart, leaving an upside down smile in its wake. Peace evaporates. Emptiness ensues. Day after day, year after year, the search for peace and purpose in life turns up only empty alleys with dusty dead-end signs.

Seeking God by works always leads to an impossibly navigable maze and confusion on which way to turn next. For example, just a few short years ago in Israel, the rabbinical authorities added a list of 150 formerly unconsidered things to those foods that were not kosher. Upon reading the news, my thoughts mused, "Did God forget something?" Of course not. God didn't forget anything. Man, in his zeal to show piety, simply reasoned that making the task harder would bring the elusive peace that was sought.

Such are the tensions and uncertainties that are the continuous companions of the one who tries to please a perfect and holy God with their own flawed righteousness. In such a field, the seeds of hopelessness eventually take root and bring forth only fruits of despair. Peace is lost amongst the weeds and thorns.

But Christians, you say, are saved by grace and believing on Jesus Christ as Lord. And to this I agree with a heart full of praise! Thank God that it is so. I too am among their brothers, and Jesus Christ is Lord in my own heart. But why is it then that, after salvation through believing on the Son of God, we sometimes become again enslaved to the lure of works? Does grace need help in winning our approval before God? No. We are saved by grace alone through faith. As the Apostle Paul reasons with us in Romans 11:6,

"And if by grace, then it cannot be based on works; if it were, grace would no longer be grace." NIV

It seems we get it half right. We acknowledge that we are saved by grace through God's mercy, and rejoice in that. But then, we slowly drift back to a heart that seeks acceptance through works; much like our Jewish friends. This too, leads to bitterness and despair. You begin to think that this is what God requires of you. But such is not the case. As much as you might take offense, the truth is that you are a very little child of His. He knows that you're just learning about the new life you've been born-again into. And He is patiently teaching you His ways. In all this, His love for you is constant and sure; even in your misunderstandings of His heart.

It's certainly the nature of man to try to achieve reward through effort. "Clean up your room, and you can have dessert.", we heard as children. "Come in on schedule, and you'll get a bonus.", we learned as adults. In the world, work earns benefit. To its citizens, that rule is as sure as gravity. Yet, contrary to all we are taught in the world, that's not how God's Kingdom works. But rather,

"Believe in the Lord Jesus, and you will be saved, you and your household."

Acts 16:31 NASB

In fact, out of all that can be said on the subject of salvation, the end of it all must be this: We are saved entirely by the atoning blood and righteousness of God's Messiah, Jesus Christ. Any attempt to trust on your own good works to provide entry to Heaven, in whole or in part, shows a complete misunderstanding of the sin condition.

There are certain spiritual realities, revealed in Scripture, that cannot be ignored. Consider God's attitude toward sin. God is perfect, and He cannot tolerate sin. He has also committed Himself to judging sin. As He told the prophet Ezekiel in Ezekiel 18:20,

"The soul who sins shall die." NKJV

God does not delight in judging man. In fact, in His mercy He has made the way for man to be saved from judgement. He knows that any sin that is before Him will be destroyed by His perfect righteousness in much the same way that light destroys the darkness. Since that sin exists in the lives of mankind, then mankind would be destroyed when the sin inside is destroyed. In this way, sin is like a disease that spreads throughout a person's life. And the sin disease is always fatal; resulting in eternal separation from God and His Kingdom.

Furthermore, God also states that all mankind has sinned; we all stand guilty before God. Romans 3:10, in the New Testament, confirms the Old Testament passages from Isaiah 53 and Psalm 14 when it says,

Romans 3:10
"There is no one righteous, not even one." NIV

Isaiah 53:6
"We all, like sheep, have gone astray, each of us has turned to our own way; and the Lord has laid on Him the iniquity of us all." NIV

Psalm 14:2-3
"The Lord looks down from heaven on all mankind to see if there are any who understand, any who seek God.

All have turned away, all have become corrupt; there is no one who does good, not even one." NIV

NOTE: Perhaps we should, at this point, explain our use of Biblical Scripture to validate what is said here. The reason why we rely on Scripture to accurately represent the thoughts of God all comes down to prophesy. There is no other book like the Bible that has accurately predicted future events. The many detailed prophecies in its pages speak of events that were far in the future when those predictions were written. And yet, those prophesies came to pass precisely as they were written.

Since no one knows the future perfectly except for God, it becomes obvious that those prophetic writings are from God. Prophesy refutes the skeptics that claim the Bible has no authority to represent God's words. In fact, fulfilled prophesy establishes the Bible as the Word of God. It makes its message inescapable and singularly important to mankind.

As we have stated, since God has committed Himself to judging all sin, and that the result of sin is death, no man can stand in His presence. God's righteousness and holiness would require the punishment for sin to be carried out upon that person. And, since all have sinned and fallen short of the glory of God, no man would escape judgment for his sins. All would perish, and there are no loopholes through which we might avoid judgement.

Jesus, Himself, in Matthew 5:48, closes the door to any other perceived defenses,

"Therefore you shall be perfect, just as your Father in heaven is perfect." NKJV

So you can see that any mix of good and sin in your life would still leave you lacking. Only the perfectly righteous person can stand before a perfect and holy God. And that's where the most important person in the Bible comes in. That's where God's role and plan for His Messiah enters the story.

God, of course, knew the sin situation. Since He had committed Himself to judging sin, He could not just forgive the unrighteousness and ignore the penalty. That would have been against His own Word and just nature.

So how could God be merciful to the sinner and yet still be just? There was only one way. God Himself would become a man and live a life keeping His own law at every moment. In that way, He would be an acceptable, blemish-free sacrifice for sin as His law had required. No other person who had ever lived qualified to be such a sacrifice, because all had sinned and fallen short of the glory of God.

But, when God's Son, Jesus Christ (who is One with the Father) came and took the punishment for our sins on Himself, all our unrighteousness was paid for. The sin had been atoned for. The penalty had been paid. Justice had been satisfied. In the Book of Isaiah the prophet, the Lord had stated that by His (The Messiah's) stripes we are healed. And with all our sins being covered by His blood, we are counted righteous before God. All who believe on God's Messiah, Jesus Christ, will be saved.

When God looks at those who believe on His Son, He sees a completely righteous person; a person whose every sin is atoned for. You become accepted to stand in the presence of the Holy God because you no longer have any sin. Your sins have been covered by the blood of the blemish-free Lamb of God.

Jesus the Messiah took our sins on Himself as the Scriptures in Isaiah 53:5 had foretold about 700 years earlier,

"But he was pierced for our transgressions, he was crushed for our iniquities; the punishment that brought us peace was on him, and by his wounds we are healed." NIV

But, in taking all our sins upon Himself, He had no sin of His own. So death could not hold Him. Remember that death is the result of sin. Since the Son of God was sinless in His own life, He was raised from the dead and is now at the right hand of the Father where He makes intercession for us.

The perfect beauty of God's plan for salvation is that both His requirement for justice and His desire to give mercy were met on the cross of the Messiah. And that is why the person of the Messiah is the most important individual in all of God's Word. Mankind's eternal welfare and salvation were on His shoulders.

Remember, that sin entered the world through man, and it had to be atoned for through man. And yet, as the Scriptures stated, all had sinned. So there was no man who was sinless to qualify as the blemish-free sacrifice for sin which had been modeled in the Passover law. God saw the need for a sinless sacrifice and designed a plan to rescue man.

God Himself would became a man and live a sinless life so that He would qualify to give His life for mankind according to His own rules. And having atoned for the sins of mankind on the cross, He has provided entry into the Kingdom of Heaven for all who simply believe on Him and the work He did on the cross. Such is the love and tender forgiveness of God.

This is the very story pictured in the Passover story in Exodus 12 where God commanded the people of Israel to take a blemish-free lamb and sacrifice it before His judgement on Egypt. He told the Hebrew people to take some of the blood from the perfect sacrificial lamb and put it on the "mezuzot" (Hebrew for "doorposts") of each of their dwellings.

Then He said in Exodus 12:13,

"... Now the blood shall be a sign for you on the houses where you are. And when I see the blood, I will pass over you; and the plague shall not be on you to destroy you when I strike the land of Egypt." NKJV

He specified a "blemish-free" lamb must be used for the sacrifice. Jesus, His Messiah, was sinless and had kept God's Law at all times. So He was "blemish-free", or free from sin. Jesus the Messiah was also sacrificed before God's judgement in the same way the Passover lamb was sacrificed before the Judgement in Exodus 12. And, as the blood of the Passover lamb protected the Hebrew people from God's judgement, the blood of Jesus the Messiah on the heart of the believer saves that person from God's coming judgement of sin.

The Passover Story is the story of God's Messiah. It spoke in detail of the Messiah's atoning death on the cross over 1,400 years before it would happen. Today, over 3,400 years later, the story is still retold in Jewish homes. Soon they will understand its meaning and recognize God's loving plan. All those years after the Exodus account, the

Son of God gave His life for the sins of mankind as Passover had foretold. And, now, all who believe on the work that God did on their behalf through the Messiah will be saved.

Again the verse at the beginning of this chapter specifies exactly what must be done to be saved,

"Jesus answered and said to them, 'This is the work of God, that you believe in Him whom He sent."

John 6:29 NKJV

Does that simple belief in the Son of God describe your life? Or are you trying to somehow combine the work of God with your own works? Many people have the idea that if they live a pretty good life, doing good deeds from time to time, they will be able to get into Heaven. But God's Kingdom is not a democracy where living 51% or more of your life doing good will gain you entry to Heaven.

As stated earlier, God is perfect, and His standard is perfect righteousness. Since He has lovingly provided the way for man's sins to be forgiven, there is no excuse for trying to stand before Him in your own unrighteousness. Salvation is from God alone. The key is relying and trusting on Him alone for acceptance before God. And that acceptance is the free gift of God to all who will ask.

As the Scripture states in the famous passage of John 3:16,

"For God so loved the world that He gave His only begotten Son, that whoever believes in Him should not perish but have everlasting life." NKJV

The person who ignores God's salvation by not believing on God's Messiah, Jesus Christ, has condemned himself. Anything less than complete dependence on God will fall short. If you insist that God look at your own good works, then He will also look at your own failures. But if you rely on the blood of the blemish-free Lamb of God alone, your sins are completely covered by His atoning sacrifice.

God desires for all to come to Him by Jesus Christ and be saved, but many refuse to come to God at all. So they are left in a sinful state in which their own sins will ultimately prevent them from receiving everlasting life in the Kingdom of Heaven.

However, for those who believe on Jesus Christ, there is no condemnation. Their sins are forgiven; not by the law of commandments, but by the law of grace through faith in God. No greater mistake could be made than relying on your own good works to try to get you into Heaven. Try as you may, you will simply never be perfectly good ... in your actions, your thoughts, and your words. The only way is to say, "Lord, I believe on Jesus Christ Your Son. Come into my heart. I want Your Righteousness. Not Mine."

CHAPTER 5
"HIS STRENGTH. NOT MINE."

"This is the Word of the Lord to Zerubbabel, 'Not by might nor by power, but by My Spirit,' says the Lord of hosts. "

Zechariah 4:6 NKJV

When memories visit from time to time, they bring their luggage. As they sit and converse with you, the luggage is opened and the contents examined. Sights, along with their textures, sounds and scents, escape their confinement and playfully revisit the senses as stories are relived. In their excitement they sometimes spill a smile on the face of the rememberer.

I recall a younger man I used to know. He had a different color of hair than the diminishing locks that struggle to hide my current head. Oh, and a trimmer profile … that younger man.

He had only recently given his life to the Lord, all those decades ago, and was fascinated with knowing more about his Creator. An amateur astronomer by aspiration, he would pack his 7 foot telescope (big boy toy) into his hippie style Volkswagen van and lug the 325 LB instrument to the nearby desert. There he would camp for a couple of nights peering into the wonders of the universe above.

The small pup tent offered no refuge from the cold desert night, but seemed rather to invite the chilled bitter wind inside. Still the treasures perused in the night skies were reward enough. Having been directed there by the ancient roadmap in Psalm 19:1, he took in the sights that painted the power of God for all to see.

"The heavens declare the glory of God; the skies proclaim the work of His hands." NIV

All night long, the pages of creation's testimony would turn above him as if singing the praises of the Creator.

When reluctantly confined to the city lights, where others seldom gaze upward, he would study the wonders he had seen. He and his friend would spend hours discussing such fascinating topics as Newtonian and Relativistic physics. They studied magazines (remember those?) where a relatively few photographs of the night skies dwelt prior to the invasion of the internet. The photos of the galaxies too numerous to number held the viewer captive.

Those were quiet days when words were inadequate. Awe became a lifestyle. They were times of contemplating the unimaginable power and majesty of God's hand. They were the nights of discovering the handiwork of the Creator of heaven and earth.

Those days, so long ago, spoke volumes to me about the power of God. When I examined the sights enveloping this tiny speck of dust in space called earth, it reminded me that nothing is impossible for God. The tiny problems we face, themselves must face the unlimited power of the Creator Who cares for me and calls me His child.

His strength is unfathomable. His power irresistible. In the end, what do I really have to fear? If He is for me then who can be against me? Any battle that comes against me would meet not my strength but His might. His guarantee to me: that no weapon formed against me will prosper. He would even cause any, and all, evil against me to work out for the good. I am protected. I am watched over. I am loved by the Creator of all things. My smile remains.

My mind has fallen off the peak of the highest mountain of imagination. It plunges gently into the ocean of eternity as thoughts of how wonderful God is, like clouds, flow overhead in praise. I am astonished that He would call me His child.

Now consider your own strength in life. There are days when you feel strong. But, there are also those days when the facts argue against those feelings. Imagination can be a friend or a foe. A misleading thought resulting in a false security in one's own strength can be tragic. But the contemplation of God's power directing and protecting your steps brings peace and security.

Just as man's wisdom is a false hope, man's strength is likewise inadequate to face the trials of life. Our strength is certainly no match for the enemies of God with whom we battle in the spiritual realm. But the Spirit of God is He Who tears down the strongholds of the enemy. He is the One Who effortlessly shatters the forces arrayed against us. It is Holy Spirit Who gives the victory.

The Holy Spirit is the One Jesus said will be with you and shall be in you. His presence overcomes all obstacles. With Him in your life, no weapon formed against you will prosper. He is your strength. When you are weak, His presence in you lifts you up and makes you to stand. He gives you overwhelming strength to carry on and to overcome. You are more than a conqueror through Him Who loves you.

Even when you feel too exhausted to continue, He changes the situation, and somehow you find strength to navigate safely through the trials.

That's why the Scriptures state in 2 Corinthians 12:10,

"For when I am weak, then I am strong." NKJV

As your own failed strength spills carelessly from your cup, God fills it with His irresistible, all powerful strength. When we acknowledge our lack of strength and our need for Him, He gently catches us in our fall and sets us safely on the ground. He is the strong fortress that we may run to and find safety. He establishes our feet on an immovable rock and puts His hand over us to shield us from anything the enemy could send our way. Oh that we would know the sweet fellowship of the Holy Spirit and be thankful for His presence and His strength in our daily lives.

When we consider God's strength for our lives, we are also reminded of His power. Though the two words are certainly strongly related, there are subtle differences in their meanings. A quick study of the two words reveals the differences.

Let's examine the words briefly.

In the context of this chapter, the Merriam-Webster Dictionary defines the word "Strength" as ...

- the quality or state of being physically strong
- the ability to resist being moved or broken by a force
- the quality that allows someone to deal with problems in a determined and effective way

The word "strength" therefore, says that God is strong. But you knew that, right? He is after all, God Almighty, the Maker of Heaven and Earth. But, when you consider the word, "strong", you probably are focused more on physical strength. Physical strength is important in the physical realm. But did you know that God is also strong in the spiritual realm where the mighty angels dwell? His strength is supreme in both the physical and spiritual realms. Both are subject to His might and nothing can stand against His will.

That's what the second part of the definition above says. He cannot be moved or broken by any force or anything. His strength is both irresistible and immovable.

Finally, and here's the one you'll really like, He can deal with your problems in a determined and effective way. In other words, the Creator who calls you His child, is the One who intercepts the problems you face and deals with them with determination to get the job done effectively. That means, when He stands between trouble and you, trouble loses ... every time.

Likewise, the word, "Power", is defined as ...

- the ability to act or produce an effect
- the legal or official authority, capacity, or right to do something

The first part of that definition confirms that the All Powerful God has the ability to take any action He desires. And, when He takes that action, it will always produce the desired effect.

So you see, not only can God do whatever He wants, but whatever He does always produces the desired effect. He also has the absolute authority and the righteous right to take the actions He deems necessary. When He acts, not only are His actions irresistible and completely effective, but they are also within His unquestionable authority as the Creator of all things.

It is both His strength and His power that He brings to bear in your life. You are His child. He desires that you go through life fearing nothing and resting in His strength at all times. It saddens Him when He sees you in fear of the things around you. He wants you to be free from fear and to realize that He is always with you. He is the One who made all those things that surround you. He is the One who has given them the boundaries that they may not cross. It is God Who is in control of all the factors that you might be tempted to fear. Your Heavenly Father is in control of all things. You can rest, child of God.

As you no doubt have noticed, the world would have you believe that God and the devil are equal in power; fighting a great battle for control of creation. Nothing could be further from the truth. In reality, the enemy of God, though formerly an angel of light and now a fallen angel of darkness, is a created being. He was created by God. Having been lifted up in his own pride, He was forced out of heaven and cast down to the earth. Now, he knows his time is short, and that judgment and the lake of fire are his end. So in futility he attempts to fight against God.

But God is the Creator of all things. His power, knowledge and wisdom are limitless. He spoke all things into existence by His Word. In a blink of His eye, God could turn all the demons into ashes and scatter them to the edges of the universe. There is no wisdom, counsel or might that can stand against the Lord. He alone is God. He alone is the all-powerful Creator of all things. From Him, and for Him and to Him are all things.

So what can the enemies of God do to hurt Him? The answer is that God's enemies can do nothing to hurt Him specifically. So instead, they spend their time trying to destroy those who God loves ... mankind. And since man was created with the ability to make his own choices in life, many are deceived by the enemies of God. They are convinced to not seek God for the salvation that could give them everlasting life. In not choosing God's salvation in Jesus the Messiah, many perish in their sins.

Of course, when man ignores the free gift of everlasting life given in Jesus Christ, God's heart breaks. He is not willing for any to perish, but for all to come to repentance and be with Him eternally in Heaven. He freely extends the invitation to all to believe on His Son and be saved.

Thus, God waits patiently for all who will come. But the time for waiting must soon end so that sin can be removed from creation and the Kingdom of God ushered in. The days are short. God must judge sin and destroy it in order to bring creation back to its original, sinless state in which He, Himself, will dwell with man eternally. In that day God will wipe away all tears, and suffering and sin and death shall be no more. So you see, there is a battle for the souls of mankind raging behind the scenes. The enemy of God cares only to destroy you, but God seeks to love you and save you and bless you eternally.

God's enemies are much smarter than you, and they can easily defeat you through deception. Daily, men fall to the lies of the enemy and go through life ignoring the very salvation that can save them. Without God in your life, no amount of human wisdom or strength can protect you from the enemies of your soul.

Sure, there are times when you feel strong. But your feelings of excitement and resolve come and go. Your mountain top confidence is soon tested on the other side of the mountain as you descend into the valleys. And the sunshine may soon be obscured by the dark clouds that always seem to develop. You may feel strong and resolute, but trusting in your own power will always bring failure.

In your own strength, you will not be able to open the doors through which God is calling you. Without the special strength He gives, you will faint along the way as your own power fades, and finally fails you. But when you come face to face with your own failings and limitations, then in brokenness, ask God for His strength in life.

He knows you need His help, and He is ready and willing to provide it. Remember, to humble yourself, and God's hand will lift you up. Your human strength is frail, and it is never enough to face those storms that come your way. So now you see your need for something more. Now you understand your need for God's supernatural strength in life. But how does one have God's strength working in their life?

The Book of Isaiah the prophet, in Isaiah 40:31, reveals the secret of going through life with unfailing, overcoming strength. Consider its promise,

"But they that wait upon the Lord shall renew their strength; they shall mount up with wings as eagles; they shall run, and not be weary; and they shall walk, and not faint." KJV

Isn't that the kind of strength you need? Human strength, like youth, fades away and leaves you searching for options. But the strength that God gives is continually renewed. Even the struggle to make it through life disappears. Instead of flapping your wings in a panic to fight against the wind and the waves you face, you can soar above your troubles. God will give you spiritual wings like an eagle. All you need to do is simply extend those wings, and the very winds that troubled you will now lift you far above the dangers and take you away to serenity.

This is the inheritance of a child of God. In all these things, your strength will be found in the Holy Spirit of God. The answers will never be in your own might or wisdom. But, as the verse that we began this chapter with confirms,

"This is the Word of the Lord to Zerubbabel, 'Not by might nor by power, but by My Spirit,' says the Lord of hosts. "

Zechariah 4:6 NKJV

No matter what your situation ... No matter what your limitations ... No matter what you've done or where you've been, God can, and will, use you. He knows your weaknesses and your shortcomings, and there is nothing in the thoughts of your heart that are hidden from Him. He knows you lack strength. And yet, the Creator of all things desires to use you in His high and noble calling.

You may not feel like you have much to give Him; that your strength has faded. But remember, He made the heavens and the earth from nothing. There's a message in the creation story especially for you today. God can take nothing and turn it into anything.

From this day onward, you will no longer fear the darkness and the uncertainty surrounding you. From this time forward you will walk in peaceful purpose; empowered not by your own abilities, but by the strength and might of the Creator of all things. Now is your time to shine. Hear His words to you, "Let there be light!" Life will now be faced in His Strength ... Not Yours.

CHAPTER 6
"HIS LOVE. NOT MINE."

"And we have known and believed the love that God has for us. God is love, and he who abides in love abides in God, and God in him."

1 John 4:16 NKJV

There are memories of events in life, and there are memories of people. Every time I think of my wonderful wife, which is often, my heart nearly stops as it looks upward and outward past my chin and smiles lovingly. I truly am truly blessed. Of course, I have also been blessed to know many others who make it their calling to hand out free smiles along life's way. Those who bring God's hope are the happiest people on earth. Sure, they have trials from time to time, but they are always looking to encourage others. God makes it His business to build things up. He creates stuff. Really cool stuff. He's not in the demolition business. He's in the construction business. Along with the universe, He also speaks peace and hope into existence in the hearts of those who trust Him. Like Him, those who are His children always have something good to say; or at least they aspire to.

But there are certain other folks, let's call them "kindness-challenged", who can be really difficult to get along with. The people they speak with usually look for opportunities to end the conversation rather quickly and be about other business. While the friendlier people are easy to love as God commanded, the latter category ... well, not so much.

To them, every conversation is a debate to win. Every person is an opponent to subdue. Everyone who attempts to take the high road must be brought to a lower level to avoid comparisons. But still, God tells us to love others; them too.

So how can you honestly say you love those who make it their goal to dislike you? A dilemma is hereby presented. It would seem that loving those who seem "unlovable" is impossible. But, perhaps that's because we don't understand what kind of love God is talking about.

In fact, there are three types of love. What? Yes, three. There is a worldly type of love we use when we say things like, "I really love chocolate ice cream!" (which, by the way, is true). That type of love holds no noble purpose or lofty thought of selflessness. It's really just a carnal love; showing only attraction to something that tickles the senses and satisfies the desire for something sweet after a meal (or before?).

Then, there's a second type of worldly love. And, while this love travels on a little higher road, it's still centered around selfishness. It's a love "of convenience"; given only on the condition that the other person involved returns the gesture and some type of mutual benefit is realized. If, however, the other person involved does not measure up to expectations, then the "love" arrangement is cancelled.

The third type of love is God's love. It's unique in that it's an unconditional love. In other words, it's given to those who don't necessarily deserve it. It's a one-way love that is given regardless of the reaction of the person to whom it is sent. The interesting thing about this type of love is that it melts the adversity in the heart of the recipient and inspires the same type of love in the person's own heart. It plants a seed that produces love in return. After a time of weeding and watering for its protection and growth, the seed breaks through the hardened surface and reaches toward the light. The love can then grow, flourish, and spread.

You'll find it impossible to love difficult people with the world's kind of love. But God's love not only loves the hardened hearts it encounters, it seeks them out. Like

light shining into a dark place, God's love melts away the
darkness. It binds up the broken hearts. It frees the
captives. It gives hope to the broken. It's delivered with a
smile and a genuine heart of compassion. It brings the
good news that those in despair seek.

It's God's love that, like x-rays, sees through the exterior
and into the heart. It pays no attention to the outward
appearance but rather looks at the inner needs. It
diagnoses the internal condition and provides the cure.
When you see the difficult person through God's eyes,
your defensive posture is replaced by humility and
understanding. That's because you yourself were a person
in need of such love in times gone by. You have been a
recipient of His love, and now His seed is producing fruit in
you.

Loving others in God's love is not only a good way to
disarm contention and soften the heart, it's also one of the
two most important commandments given by God. In
Matthew 22:35-40 we read of its importance,

*One of them, a lawyer, asked Him a question, testing
Him, "Teacher, which is the great commandment in the
Law?" And He said to him, " 'You shall love the Lord
your God with all your heart, and with all your soul, and
with all your mind.' "This is the great and foremost
commandment. "The second is like it, 'You shall love your*

neighbor as yourself.' "On these two commandments depend the whole Law and the Prophets." NASB

The short story of this passage is the very heartbeat of life. It's vital that we consider its message and paint each word and action of life with its colors and textures. The first thing we notice is that God commands us to love. We are to love Him with all that we are. And we are to love mankind who is made in His image. No exceptions.

Jesus Himself said that the first commandment about loving God is the greatest and foremost commandment. It certainly is much easier to love God; given His unconditional love for us, given His perfection and righteousness. But Jesus also said the second commandment, the one about loving others, is like the first commandment. That means it's of like importance to love others. Yes, loving others is not just a good thing to do. It's commanded that we do it.

And yet, if you love others (including the difficult ones) reluctantly ... only because you are commanded to do so, you're not truly loving them. Your heart's not in it. You're not truly concerned about their hopelessness. You're just going through the motions.

Sadly, there are also people who "love" others only to make them feel ashamed ... only to subdue them with humiliation. But the goal of God's love is not that others might suffer, but that they would be saved. The goal of God's love is to soften the hardened heart and melt the ice surrounding it. The motivation in bringing God's love is to bring about well-being and tenderness in the heart of the hearer. The result we seek is not a punished person, but a new creature who is released from the cruel prison of sin. We seek to see the face of the person beholding the goodness of God and changed by His light.

Learning to love other people with God's love is not a laborious task. It need not take weeks or months or years to learn. There are not "10 Easy Steps to Loving with God's Love" books that you need to read. You can begin today. All you have to do is revisit what you already know.

Consider how God loved you. Think for a moment about how He sought you out. In relentless pursuit He tracked you down and confronted you with the story of His incredible love for you. Briefly remember the awful list of transgressions He looked past and forgave in order to draw you into His family. Your sins, which were many, have been forgiven. Now, go and do likewise.

Take a moment to look carefully at a story much like your own in Luke 7:36-47,

Then one of the Pharisees asked Him to eat with him. And He went to the Pharisee's house, and sat down to eat. And behold, a woman in the city who was a sinner, when she knew that Jesus sat at the table in the Pharisee's house, brought an alabaster flask of fragrant oil, and stood at His feet behind Him weeping; and she began to wash His feet with her tears, and wiped them with the hair of her head; and she kissed His feet and anointed them with the fragrant oil.

Now when the Pharisee who had invited Him saw this, he spoke to himself, saying, "This Man, if He were a prophet, would know who and what manner of woman this is who is touching Him, for she is a sinner."

And Jesus answered and said to him, "Simon, I have something to say to you." So he said, "Teacher, say it."

"There was a certain creditor who had two debtors. One owed five hundred denarii, and the other fifty. And when they had nothing with which to repay, he freely forgave them both. Tell Me, therefore, which of them will love him more?"

Simon answered and said, "I suppose the one whom he forgave more."

And He said to him, "You have rightly judged." Then He turned to the woman and said to Simon, "Do you see this woman? I entered your house; you gave Me no water for My feet, but she has washed My feet with her tears and wiped them with the hair of her head. You gave Me no kiss, but this woman has not ceased to kiss My feet since the time I came in. You did not anoint My head with oil, but this woman has anointed My feet with fragrant oil. Therefore I say to you, her sins, which are many, are forgiven, for she loved much. But to whom little is forgiven, the same loves little." NKJV

You see, the one who has been forgiven much loves much, but the one who has been forgiven little loves little. In other words, the worse that person you're speaking to is, the more they will love God after they experience His love through you. God desires to use you to illustrate His compassion and patience to those He brings across your path.

Consider, again, your own story. You were imprisoned in a dark, filthy, confined and infested prison. You had become so familiar with your surroundings that you just viewed the situation as normal. You had long since lost all hope of ever getting out. You just resigned yourself to thinking this is how it's going to be. You even became somewhat comfortable in your cruel captivity. But one day, the Son of a distant King and His soldiers defeated your captors and opened your prison door, setting you free. At first the bright light of freedom seemed too much. You had become accustomed to the darkness. But in time, your eyes became adjusted to the light. You would just stand outside and stare for the longest times at the things you had not been able to see before. The vivid colors you beheld were the very messengers that exclaimed your new freedom. Having been imprisoned by sin for all those years, you were now free!

Previously, you had been a prisoner of despair and hopelessness, but now you were captured by love. The benevolent King of Kings had sent His Son to rescue you. Oh, how you loved that King who had set you free; how you loved His Son. How you wished to know everything you could about Him. Now you sought to proclaim His compassion to others in darkness that they, too, might be free. You are now His. You were captured by His love.

Loving others is so important that it is the single quality that proves that you are God's child. It's your credentials; proving you are a citizen of the Kingdom of Heaven. In John 13:35, Jesus shows it as the one thing that identifies a person as His follower ...

"By this all men will know that you are My disciples, if you have love for one another." NASB

Again, we see God's emphasis on the supreme importance of love. God Himself is love, and the one who loves is born of God and knows God. His nature is the very personification of love. That well known verse in John 3:16 states God's motivation in saving mankind. Set your eyes intently on it and thoughtfully consider each and every word. The key to eternity is contained within it. It says,

"For God so loved the world that He gave His only begotten Son, that whoever believes in Him should not perish but have everlasting life." NKJV

Indeed, God revealed to us what true love is, and we love Him because He first loved us. Shouldn't we also love others in the same way?

But, as we said earlier, sometimes it's difficult to love some people. There's a variety of reasons we present to attempt to disqualify various people we should show compassion to. They might have done things you did not approve of. Or they may have said bad things about you. They may even have tried to hurt you; or a hundred other reasons why you don't feel you could ever love them.

But God makes it clear that we are to love others; period. He will sort out all the other issues about worthiness and what those people did with His love. But you are commanded to love them. Remember to see them with their needs and not with their angry and hurtful words. See them through your Heavenly Father's eyes. Think on His patience. Persist. Be relentless in your love for them. You don't know the effect your compassion will have on their hearts. You may one day see the change that God wrought in their life. Then you will rejoice. Or you may never see that person again, but one day their heart will be changed because of how you, and other believers, showed compassion. It is also a possibility that person may never respond to the love of God. Each person has been created with the ability to choose. That's what makes our love for God genuine and not merely a programmed response. Still, in any case, we are called to love others. Plant your seeds as you travel along life's road. The love shown us by God constrains us to do so. The beautiful passage in 1 John 4:11 states,

"Dear friends, since God so loved us, we also ought to love one another."

So it remains ... We are to love God with all our being, and we are also to love one another. Remember 1 John 4:7,

"Beloved, let us love one another: for love is of God; and everyone that loves is born of God, and knows God."
                                                                    NKJV

How many times have you asked, "Why am I here? What's my calling in life?" The concise answer is that you are here to love God and to show His love to others. It's that simple! You have a message that angels cannot share. You have a story, your testimony, of God's compassion to you, yourself a sinner, now saved by grace. God could have taken you to be with Him immediately after you gave your life to Him. After all, if He had you would not have had another opportunity to sin. Right? The reason why you were left on earth is to tell other people, who need to know, how God's compassion saved you. God wants you to show others His love by loving them.

"Okay", you say, "but what does that mean?" Well, let's rewind the memories a bit. Do you remember that person you passed by the other day … the one that looked hopeless and hurting … the one who had that blank stare looking nowhere in particular? The one who seemed to be wrestling with their very survival? Did you feel your heart strings tugging at your hands to do something? Was your innermost being telling your mouth to say something? That's what love looks like. Your heart was trying to carry your feet to a place where you could show God's love.

Now, showing God's love is not simply talking. The message is far more effective when love is demonstrated. I heard someone once say, "Love is something you do." It's not something simply spoken of. It's not meant to be a theological debate topic or even the words of a book. Love can be a noun, but in much of the context of the Bible, it's a verb … a word of action. Love truly is something you do. It is the immovable ground upon which your theological doctrine stands. It proves the truth of what your mouth speaks.

Demonstrating God's love involves sacrifice. Love without sacrifice is accepted only in legalistic minds. But love with sacrifice is powerful, denying standing to all who would otherwise debate your sincerity and message.

You may be on your way to somewhere else at the time when God schedules that unexpected divine appointment. Is your schedule flexible enough to take the diversion? You may be very tired, and just wanting to rest. Then God brings that person who, for some strange reason, begins to pour out their heart to you and explain what's happening in their life. The calling for some of God's children is simply to listen and show interest. Is that you? Can you put your own plans and desires on hold for a little bit to smile hope to the hopeless or listen to those who have nobody?

Have you been praying for God to use you? Could this be how He answers that prayer? Are you available for Him to use? As I said before, out of all the abilities you think you might bring to a ministry, the only one He truly desires is your "avail-ability". Are you available?

Love is most powerful and most clearly seen in the setting of sacrifice. That hurting friend or stranger understands that God's love is speaking to them when they see selflessness and sacrifice in your actions.

After all, God's love was painted richly upon our hearts in the image of the sacrifice of His Son. You are His child. In a way, you could say that you have His "spiritual DNA". In other words, you have the capacity to consider things in your heart that are in His heart. Your Heavenly Father is working amongst those around you. You should also be about your Father's business.

In Matthew 10:8 Jesus said,

"Freely you have received. Freely give." NKJV

You have received an unconditional love. Now reach out to others and give them that kind of love. Show God's love to them that they too may be drawn to Him; that they also may know the hope He offers.

In John Chapter 4, Jesus had just completed a walk of at least 20 miles from Aenon in Judah to a spot near the town of Sychar in Samaria. He was tired and weary from the journey, and He stopped at a well near the town. There He saw a Samaritan woman who had come to the well to draw water. She would come to draw the water from the well then carry the heavy containers back to the town. There was nobody to help her.

Normally the people would have come to the well in the coolness of the day. They would have come together to help each other and to socialize with each other a bit. But this woman had come alone. There was a reason. She was an outcast from the town's society. In the town, she had a shady reputation. She had been married five times before, and the man she was now living with was not her husband. No doubt the people of the town would say, "Stay away from her. She's trouble." So, she came to the well alone.

When Jesus saw her, He asked her for a drink of water from the well. He had no container to put down into the well. She did. Sure, He was thirsty, but there was a more important reason He had stopped at that particular well near that particular town. He had been guided there by the Holy Spirit for a very important divine appointment.

When the woman heard Jesus ask her for a drink, she was astonished that He spoke to her. The Jews at that time had very little regard for the Samaritans. They normally didn't speak to them at all. It was even stranger for a Jewish man to speak to a Samaritan woman. She began talking to Jesus about how strange it was that He was speaking to her. As they talked, Jesus quickly guided the conversation to speak of things pertaining to the Kingdom of God. He told her of the living water that He would give to those who ask Him. He said that those who drink of this living water would never thirst again.

When she expressed interest in the living water He spoke of, He told her to go and get her husband. She replied that she was not married; trying to hide the real situation behind unblinking eyes. But Jesus already knew all the details of her life. He then recounted the details of her marriages and the current situation to her as she listened in a mixture of amazement and shame.

Yes, it was very embarrassing; true. But there was also something incredible happening there, and she sensed it. He knew of her sinful lifestyle with all the husbands and the man she was living with, yet He did not judge her for those sins. For Him, the most important thing was to bring the message of forgiveness of sins and eternal life.

She reasoned that He was a prophet, so she started talking about religion and even spoke of the Messiah who everyone knew was coming sometime soon. That's when Jesus told her something He had never said before and that she would not forget. He told her that He is the Messiah! She ran in excitement back to the town and told everybody about Him. Yes, even those people who had previously shunned her. She told everyone about Jesus.

Suddenly, for the first time in such a long time, she felt that she was part of something important; that she was really cared for by another. Suddenly she realized that God knew she existed and that He had crashed into her darkness and shone His wonderful light.

It was to this sinful, Samaritan woman of a bad reputation that Jesus had first revealed Himself to be the Messiah. She had been chosen to be the first to hear that wonderful

news. Afterward, as she went into her own city, she
proclaimed the message to the rest of people there. So
she was among the first to repeat that saving message.
And she had heard the message from the Lord Himself.
She had believed. So, of course, she would now tell others
of the wonderful love of God!

Jesus could have seen that she was a Samaritan and just
passed on by without speaking to her. Or, knowing her
sinful past, He could have decided to wait and speak to
somebody else. But God is love, and the Son of Man had
come to save sinners. So He took the time to show
compassion. He spoke to the woman who few, if any, in
the town would have cared to speak with. It was not
beneath Him to speak with her. It was exactly that
message to sinners that He was sent to bring. He was sent
to tell them that through believing on Him they could be
saved.

He was called to share God's love and proclaim the
Kingdom of God. He was called to show the compassionate
mercy and love of God to the broken, the hopeless, the
outcasts, and the despairing. The world's type of love
would cringe at outreach such as this. But God's love is
unconditional and available to all. The Messiah had come
into the world to save sinners. And now the news was out.
He had arrived! The message was now being spread.
Salvation through Him was available to all who would
believe.

As a result of Jesus showing compassion to the woman her life was changed that day. She became an evangelist; a missionary to the very city in which she had been considered a notorious sinner.

When you think about it, she was exactly the kind of person God was looking for ... a sinner saved by His grace. She was a thankful person who would go to yet others and proclaim the goodness and mercy of God. She had a story.

The Creator of the universe had spoken to her heart, "Let there be light!", and that day her life was eternally changed. A glowing smile had taken residence on her previously hopeless face. An overwhelming joy had invaded her heart and had evicted the darkness. Not only did she now have purpose in life, she had a world-changing purpose.

Her calling, that very day, would change the entire town where she resided. Many of the inhabitants would come to hear this Messiah she had spoken with, and they would choose to believe on Him. Such was the power of love when shown to even the least in society.

Who is the Samaritan of shady reputation in your city? Would you, though weary or hurried, pause to share God's love and hope with them? Who is that person who's just impossible to get along with? Would you be willing to endure their remarks and invest yet another smile in order to demonstrate God's patience and compassion toward them?

When you step forward, the Holy Spirit will step in and direct your steps and give you the right words. He will use you to reach others with God's love. All that is needed of you is a willingness to be used by Him. Are you willing? If so, He will do wonderful things through you and use you to shine His light into the darkness. It all becomes possible when you show His Love … Not Yours.

CHAPTER 7
"HIS GLORY. NOT MINE."

"For Yours is the kingdom, and the power, and the glory forever. Amen "

Matthew 6:13 NKJV

The early morning sky has invited a sleepy breeze to begin its playful journey down the streets of the city. Tiny flowers painted by the Artist's hand begin to sway back and forth in unison as if in praise. Their small leaves on the hanging vines around me appear as a great puzzle. Each piece reflects the soft morning light from a slightly different angle lending the image a gentle shimmering. The intricate stems connecting them are almost hidden under the shade of each of their tiny green umbrellas. A visiting ant speeds down their roads to destinations unknown. From the smallest creature to the tallest mountain, creation is gently reminding man of God's glory.

The whispered, yet certain, story speaks in contrast to the confused world over which it is superimposed as a vast beautiful painting overlaying a desolate field. Yet His Word of Hope speaks of an imminent day in which the failures of man will be replaced with the glory of God. This upside down world will soon be righted. Oh how I long for that day.

The world's current society, given to shallow and superficial values, measures you by your outward successes. To the world your net worth is a number with a dollar sign in front of it. Oh, and there may be a minus in there as well. How do you feel about that? It's not very encouraging, is it? Has not your real contribution in life been the things that could not be deposited in a bank account; the things that are unseen but nonetheless of great value? But such are the warped values of a world that focuses on mere temporary, decaying, and material objects.

Confused by the world's rules, it's easy to become proud of worldly accomplishments. But pride in your own efforts seems simply another way of ascribing glory to yourself. That pride in self is tragically misplaced, and leads only to destruction. For God will humble the proud, but He will exalt the lowly.

The Holy Spirit again reasons with the vain heart when He says in 1 Corinthians 4:7,

"For who makes you different from anyone else? What do you have that you did not receive? And if you did receive it, why do you boast as though you did not?" *NIV*

Strangely the world, in false confidence, proclaims that what society needs is even more self-esteem. In fact, the opposite is true. The river of our existence overflows its banks with the mud of self-esteem. The destructive results render as unimportant the value of others around us and wrestle to keep the focus stayed firmly on self. But the real need, according to God's Word, is humility. Its wisdom gently admonishes of the need to value others above ourselves. As Philippians 2:3 guides us,

"Do nothing out of selfish ambition or vain conceit, rather in humility value others above yourselves." *NIV*

We could use an extended vacation from "self-esteem". God's Kingdom turns society upside down and establishes that the greatest shall be a servant of all. We need to let our thoughts wander from the shallow issue of self importance and onto the glory of God. For this is the true purpose of life. To be in awe of, and to proclaim, His glory.

Scriptures teach us that God will not share His glory with another, and that all glory is rightfully His. It's okay to check your spiritual health from time to time, of course, but you need to take a humble view of yourself. After all, Jesus said in Luke 17:10,

"In the same way, when you obey me you should say, 'We are unworthy servants who have simply done our duty."
NLT

Don't go through life trying to fit in with a world in which you don't belong. You are in the world, but the Lord has called you out of the world. This world no longer holds the title deed over your life. You are a child of the King of Kings. You are treasured by the Lord of Lords. The One Who sits on Heaven's Throne calls you His beloved child.

Remember who you are. Remember where you're from. You are an ambassador from a distant Kingdom, sent by the King of Kings to represent Him and bring His message to a foreign land. Live life according to the values of the Kingdom of Heaven of which you are a citizen. View yourself as a servant of all according to the ways of His Kingdom.

Yes, "servant of all" means to serve even those who you don't get along with at times. If fact, your humility will be the very weapon that disarms their arguments against you. One simply cannot fight against love that is shown. Eventually, love triumphs. Christ has taken you to be His, and your life is being molded in His image. He came as a servant of all to give His life as a sacrifice to provide forgiveness of sins. Have His heart in you. Serve in humility before God each day of life in order to bring glory to your Heavenly Father.

"Guard your heart above all else, for it determines the course of your life."

Proverbs 4:23 NLT

View all that you have as from God, giving Him the glory that is rightfully His alone. Consider that every breath, every heartbeat, each new day is a gift from Him. All we have, we enjoy from His hand. It is only through His strength that you can do anything at all in life. Those who know Him are kept by Him, and even the storms of life and the valleys we travel through will turn to bless us in the end because we are His.

If you are His child, you are watched over by Him and constantly in His care. It is through His wisdom that He has directed your steps to lead you to the place that He wants you to be. When you truly understand your role in life and His love for you, you can rest and be confident that all that comes your way will turn out for the better. And walking daily in that freedom, will inspire you to praise Him.

There will be those times when all is well, and you are inspired to praise God for His goodness. It may be that He has brought a pleasant answer to a severe need you had prayed about. Maybe He brought along a blessing that you had no idea was coming. Or you just surveyed life and felt that all was in order. I like to call those times "praise jumps".

You see the goodness of God at an unexpected time or in an unexpected way, and praise suddenly wells up inside you. Your heart jumps with joy. A missing piece to the puzzle has fallen into place and with it wonderful opportunities have opened up. A smile jumps onto your face, and its trail of happy dust falls onto your heart. You've just experienced a "praise jump". The fault line that divides sadness from joy in your heart has had a "heartquake". The feeling that "it's just another day" has been replaced with a sense that a special event has just been recorded in life.

But what of those other days? You know which ones I mean. The days when, you know you should be thanking God, but things just don't seem to be going well. That problem you'd been praying about has gotten even worse. You had an unexpected setback with your job or a relationship with someone. Maybe you received news of an unexpected medical condition that stopped life in its tracks. What about those times when it just seems difficult to move ahead with a heart of praise? Can you offer genuine thanks in difficult situations when your feelings may disagree with your words? How does one continue to praise God in the valleys?

I remember a time many years ago when my feet traversed such a valley. I had received news of something that had stolen my joy; all of it. After taking inventory of my few options, my mind quickly zoomed down to the bottom line of the situation. Hopelessness, eagerly it seems, replaced my worries. Sadness invited itself into my heart on that long walk along the inner city streets of my native Dallas.

Suddenly, and completely unexpected, an uninvited thought walked through the door of my private sadness. The thought turned to me and whispered in my ear, "Start thanking God." I stepped back, "What? How can I thank God at a time like this?" I paused in brief consideration of the thought, "I would be a hypocrite." Yet, deep inside I knew that God had sent the thought. I knew it was the right thing to do. Still, I attempted to walk away from the thought, but it was stuck to my head somehow. A private conversation ensued with God. He won.

Slowly, and certainly reluctantly, I began to think of a couple of things I could thank Him for. I formed the memories into awkward words. There, I've done it, I thought. But my heart convicted me to continue. I continued for a few seconds more. But the conviction was stubbornly stuck in my flesh. With a sigh, against my better wishes, I set out for the real thing, thanking God for each thing that came to mind. That's when something strange began to happen inside me.

With each archived thought brought to my mind's display, I felt a slight tug at the ends of my lips pulling them toward the shape of a smile. Before long the tugs actually became a little painful due to all the smiling. As one memory after another of God's faithfulness played its movie trailer on my mind's screen, my current situation faded away. The pace of my steps had picked up noticeably and had a rhythm of joy in them. Before long I was thanking God out loud and amazed at His goodness as I could not stop proclaiming His glory. To this day I cannot even remember what the situation was that I had faced that day. All I know is that, whatever it was, it disappeared; dropped somewhere on the sidewalk along the way I suppose. But vivid is the memory of the lesson learned on that walk.

I have concluded that praise, even reluctant praise, gives birth to more praise. It is amazing to know that praise can heal the worrying and hurting heart. Not only are we supposed to praise God, but it is also very good for us to do so.

The darkness would have kept the memories of God's goodness deep within the prison of self-pity. But the recounting of His faithfulness overcame the guards and broke open those prison doors. The escaping stories ran to freedom, jumping for joy in their proclamation of God's goodness. Praise had overcome! Heaven joined in that day, and we all had a big joy party.

People like to think that they are generally good. They award themselves this distinction because , when they compare themselves with others, their life does not stand out as particularly evil. And when they see something they are better at than another person, they congratulate themselves and take pride in their perceived accomplishment. But those self-given awards are relative to the perceived righteousness of others and are not true righteousness.

True righteousness is not based on your relative morality compared to other people. No, true righteousness is when your actions and behavior and thoughts are perfect in God's eyes. And God is absolutely perfect, so His standard is absolute perfection. Anything in your life that has not been perfect has missed the mark that God has established so that a person can be permitted to stand in His Presence in His Kingdom. He doesn't grade on a sliding scale based on how righteous you are compared to other people.

You have, no doubt, noticed the decline in the morality, courtesy, and compassion of civilization lately. Society, having tried to deny its Creator, is in tragic decline. As society spirals downward, and human behavior degrades, the curve with which you grade yourself also becomes lower. So without realizing it you, yourself, are losing ground in your efforts to be truly good. And there is no glory due you in that.

Instead, you should give yourself to proclaiming the glory of God, our Creator. All glory rightly belongs to Him alone. But it has become unacceptable in the eyes of the world to proclaim God's glory. Indeed, in more and more places, it's become forbidden to speak of God at all. In Luke 19:40 the people of Jerusalem were beholding the Messiah coming into the city and to His temple. They responded by uttering the prophetic phrase reserved for the Messiah's coming. As Psalm 118:26 had said hundreds of years earlier,

"Blessed is He who comes in the name of the Lord."
NKJV

But there were some there who complained to Jesus that the people should refrain from offering praise. To them the Lord replied,

" ... I tell you, that if these should hold their peace, the stones would immediately cry out." Luke 19:40 KJV

I recently read a story in the news that spoke to my heart about the dangerous times in which we live. I am grateful to Fox News for reporting on the following story, the full and beautiful details of which appear in their archives.

It seems a small school in the USA had previously been sued by a student claiming duress because the school had allowed Christian activities in its facilities. In his judgement, the judge ruled in favor of the one individual and instructed the school to refrain from using any material mentioning God.

For a recent football game, the school's band had meticulously prepared a special song to perform at half-time. The song was the beautiful hymn, "How Great Thou Art" which builds to a great crescendo as it proclaims the goodness and glory of God. But, at half time, school officials reluctantly announced there would be no special half-time performance because of the recent ruling of the judge. A protracted moment of silence set in among those sitting in the seats around the event.

Then, from within the stillness, a single woman rose to her feet and began singing the hymn herself. At first her small voice was almost indistinguishable in the large crowd gathered there. But, after a short while, a few others stood to join with her in the song. Before long, hundreds had taken to their feet to join in the chorus of praise as they proclaimed to God, "How great Thou art!". No legal ruling or judge would be stopping the proclamation of

God's glory that night. The light had defeated the darkness. The stones had cried out!

You may only be a single voice in the crowd, but use that voice to proclaim the glory of God in the midst of the present darkness. Let your light shine! All creation will proclaim His glory. And all who try to silence the resounding proclamation will fail as creation sings of the glory of God.

A wonderful habit to adopt is to set aside some time to consider the faithfulness of God in your own life. Recounting His goodness to you in days gone by builds faith for today and tomorrow. It's a wonderful addition to your daily devotions and prayer times. It's a scenic retreat from the stresses and storms surrounding you. Remembering His goodness is like taking shelter in a beautiful, strong and towering fortress. The storms viewed from the castle's great windows lose their threats and become only scenic artwork in the shelter of God's care.

The glory of God is a subject that cannot be fully comprehended. Where does one start in proclaiming it? Our minds are quickly consumed in infinite splendor when trying to surround the subject in thought. But there is a single account in Scripture in which the glory of God is perfectly defined and proclaimed. I can say that with confidence because, in this passage, God's glory is proclaimed by God Himself! This remarkable passage and

its surrounding story begins in Exodus 33:18. That verse
shows Moses asking God to show him His glory. God
responds to Moses in Exodus 34:5-8,

Exodus 34:5-8 … *"Now the Lord descended in the cloud
and stood with him there, and proclaimed the name of the
Lord. 6 And the Lord passed before him and proclaimed,
"The Lord, the Lord God, merciful and gracious,
longsuffering, and abounding in goodness and truth,
7 keeping mercy for thousands, forgiving iniquity and
transgression and sin, by no means clearing the guilty,
visiting the iniquity of the fathers upon the children and
the children's children to the third and the fourth
generation."
8 So Moses made haste and bowed his head toward the
earth, and worshiped." NKJV*

Just prior to the above passage, God had told Moses that
He would pass before him and proclaim the name of the
Lord. In Hebrew, names have meanings. They speak to the
character of the one to whom the name belongs. So it's no
surprise that we see God proclaiming His name by
proclaiming the things He does and the things He values.
God is telling Moses who He is.

Remember that Moses did not have a Bible that he could
study to find out about God. God had revealed Himself to
Moses from the burning bush prior to calling him to

deliver the Hebrews from their bondage in Egypt. Moses had certainly seen the power of God manifested in the plagues that were shown against Pharaoh, but Moses, as Abraham before him, did not fully understand the heart of God yet. He did not know about the many attributes that God spoke of in the verses above.

It was in these verses that God revealed the aspects of His person that centered around compassion and mercy. But He also revealed that He judges sin. He also showed that the results of a person's sin could impact his family in future generations as well. Such is the devastating effect that sin can have on peoples' lives. All this information was completely new knowledge to Moses about the character of God.

Of course, Moses had some hints about God's mercy because He had certainly been merciful to Israel in bringing them out of Egypt. But Moses had also seen God severely punish Egypt even to the point of taking the life of every first born in the land. It's possible that Moses wondered if God would be as severe on Israel if something were amiss in their relationship with Him. So the things God reveals here in Exodus 34 about His character are very important to Moses. The things concerning mercy that were proclaimed by God, put to rest any fears that Moses may have had.

It's also interesting that all the things mentioned as God proclaims His name, are not the things that man usually thinks of when he thinks of God. We usually think of the All Powerful God who made the universe and all that is. We think of the Omni-Present God who is everywhere at the same time. We think of the God who is able to hear each person's prayers individually though multitudes may be praying around the world. We think of the manifestations of God's power in creation around us. Why didn't God proclaim those things in the description of who He is? The answer is found in Romans 1:20-21,

"Romans 1:20 For since the creation of the world His invisible attributes are clearly seen, being understood by the things that are made, even His eternal power and Godhead, so that they are without excuse, 21 because, although they knew God, they did not glorify Him as God, nor were thankful, but became futile in their thoughts, and their foolish hearts were darkened." NKJV

You see, the things pertaining to God's power and infinite wisdom were already revealed to anyone who wished to know. All they had to do was look up at the night sky and consider God's wisdom and power. His might was on display for all to see. But the things that God revealed about Himself to Moses in Exodus 34:5-8 was new information. Those things revealed the tender, compassionate and merciful heart of God. Remember, Moses had asked God to show him His glory. God had answered by proclaiming these things.

So when you are inspired to proclaim God's glory, you could use God's example as your own guidelines. Consider His tender mercies. In your own testimony, speak to others about the compassion God has shown you. Share your story of how God has forgiven your sins. Tell the story of who He is, so others may also be drawn to Him.

Throw overboard your vain attempts to establish your own fame in life. Sail away from your former false treasures. Proclaim His glory. It is the singular purpose of your life. It's the reason why God has placed you here. Spread the good news about how God has shown mercy to man. Speak with bold, contagious joy about how He will save all who accept His free gift of salvation in His Son Jesus Christ. Spend your days speaking of His wonderful works and ways. Contrary to the ways of the world, settle it in your heart to proclaim His Glory ... Not Yours.

"THE WHISPERS OF GOD"

Twelve Weeks of Hope & Renewal

"Finally, brothers and sisters, whatever is true, whatever is noble, whatever is right, whatever is pure, whatever is lovely, whatever is admirable—if anything is excellent or praiseworthy—think about such things."
Philippians 4:8 NIV

Many are the whispers of God that gently guide us. These, contained in His Word, offer peace and hope. They reveal the secrets of His Kingdom and guide those thirsty for truth to its gates. The following pages contain twelve short devotions that will bring hope to your life and remind you of God's faithfulness. Each deals with a topic that we all face from time to time. Choose one to be your companion for one week. Review it each morning without distraction as a reminder of its message. At the end of the seven days, the message will have been firmly rooted in your heart. Hope will begin to replace fear, and peace will be your faithful companion as you journey through life.

Stillness in the Storms

"And He arose and rebuked the wind, and said unto the sea, "Peace, be still." And the wind ceased and there was a great calm."

Mark 4:39 KJV

The disciples feared for their lives as the great storm tossed them about. Then Jesus said those three words, "Peace, be still." Though He spoke to the storm, He was also speaking to their troubled hearts. Listen as He whispers His words of peace and hope to you, and great calm will be yours. As long as God is with us, we are safe. And He has promised to never leave us or forsake us.

Don't let the storms in life steal your peace away. Those storms are temporary. You have been given everlasting life with the eternal Creator. All things are yours in Him. You are the doorkeeper of your own heart. You don't have to let those troubles outside you take up residence inside. Just refuse their entry and keep your heart thinking on the noble, pure and holy things of God. Soon enough those storms that worry you will fade away. The peace the Lord has given you is a peace the world can never take away. It's a peace that passes all understanding.

God Can Use Adversity to Lead You

"You intended to harm me, but God intended it for good to accomplish what is now being done, the saving of many lives."

Genesis 50:20 NIV

As a young man, Joseph's older brothers didn't like him. Eventually they turned on Joseph and sold him into slavery in Egypt just to get rid of him. In a strange land, far away from home, things didn't seem to go well for Joseph. A woman accused him of making sexual advances, and her husband had Joseph cast into jail. But Joseph didn't question God's plans. He kept on trying to do the right thing and be a man of God. One night two other prisoners had prophetic dreams that Joseph was able to interpret. Two years later Pharaoh himself had a dream and heard that Joseph could interpret it. Joseph revealed that the dream warned of a coming famine, and Pharaoh gave Joseph great authority to manage all of Egypt's food in the coming crisis. Eventually, Joseph's brothers came from Canaan to find food, and because Joseph was in a position of authority, he was able to provide them food so that they would not perish. God had used adversity to place Joseph where he needed him.

Higher Education for the Believer

"All Scripture is God-breathed and is useful for teaching, rebuking, correcting and training in righteousness, so that the servant of God may be thoroughly equipped for every good work."

2 Timothy 3:16-17 NIV

The Bible is the best selling book of all time. That's because the prophesies predicted in it come true. People realize that only God knows the future. So if the prophesies of the Bible come true, then the book must truly be from God. Now that's important because, in addition to those prophecies, the Bible gives instructions on how man can be saved and have everlasting life in Heaven. Also given are instructions for successfully navigating life itself. The words of its pages give wisdom, understanding and guidance to direct one's steps in the ways of God. In the Bible, one finds peace with their Creator and discovers how much He loves them. God's Word gives the reader peace and purpose in life. And it reveals the free gift of everlasting life that is found by believing on God's Son, Jesus Christ.

Called to Love, Not to Judge

"Do not judge others, and you will not be judged. For you will be treated as you treat others."

Matthew 7:1-2 NLT

We all have failures in life from times when we made the wrong decisions or times when we just blatantly sinned against God. And, before you gave your life to the Lord, you lacked the wisdom to truly know the difference between right and wrong. But after the Lord comes into your life, He teaches you about the tragedy of sin and His goodness in forgiving your sins. Afterward, you may be tempted to look at others, who don't yet know the Lord, and ridicule their lack of understanding. But remember that God forgave you and saved you so that He would not have to judge you. He loved you unconditionally before you ever even thought about Him. Shouldn't we look at others with the same patience, compassion and understanding? After all, a child of God should live in the example of their Heavenly Father. And reaching out in His love can be the key to introducing others to Him.

God Can Still Use You

"Jesus answered and said to her, "Whoever drinks of this water will thirst again, but whoever drinks of the water that I shall give him will never thirst. But the water that I shall give him will become in him a fountain of water springing up into everlasting life."

John 4:13-14 NKJV

The key word in the verse above is the word, "whoever". It means "anybody". That includes you. The woman Jesus was speaking to was not a prominent business leader. Nor was she a respected citizen in the town she had come from. In fact, she had a rather bad reputation. She had been married five times before, and she was currently living with a man who was not her husband. No doubt the other people in the town would say, "Stay away from her. She's trouble." But Jesus saw potential in her and spoke to her. As a result she became the first person to which He revealed Himself as the Messiah, and she went and told her whole village about Jesus. Afterward, many of them believed in Him. Your background, and all those past failures, won't stop God. He can still use you! In fact, all He needs is your availability. Are you available for God?

Honor Others Above Yourself

"Do nothing out of selfish ambition or vain conceit.
Rather, in humility value others above yourselves,"
Philippians 2:3 NIV

One day the disciples were walking along the road with
Jesus, and the Lord noticed them discussing which of them
was the greatest. They were ashamed that He had heard
them. Jesus taught that the greatest in His Kingdom
would be a servant of everyone else. The ways of the world
are exactly the opposite. In the world, people try to gain
authority over others in their quest to promote themselves.
But the Kingdom of Heaven will be inherited by the meek
... those who are humble.

The two greatest commandments in God's Word are to
love the Lord your God with all your heart, mind and
strength; and to love your neighbor as yourself. You can't
obey either of those if your actions are always about
yourself. True fulfillment in life comes from following the
Son of God's example in giving and living your life for
others. God's Kingdom turns it all upside down.

Spend Your Life Encouraging Others

"So encourage each other and build each other up, just as you are already doing."

1 Thessalonians 5:11 NLT

Many in the world try to tear others down in order to make themselves look better. The world attacks people who endeavor to live a life of integrity and goodness. All while those in the world are taught that they are mere accidents of nature. They are taught that man simply evolved more than the other species on earth; that he has no noble purpose in life. The irony is that, after they falsely teach people that they evolved from apes, they then tell the same people that they need more self-esteem. Life without God cheapens life and equates man to a mere chance combination of chemistry . Again, the way of the world is to tear people down; to make them feel worthless and helpless. But the Creator of the universe is a builder. He doesn't tear down those made in His image. He builds them up. And He has given to us the ministry of compassionately encouraging others and building them up. People need to know they were put here for a noble purpose in God's plan. Take time today to encourage someone. It will change your own life as well.

Forgive as God Has Forgiven You
" ... Remember, the Lord forgave you, so you must forgive others."

Colossians 3:13 NLT

Few things in life cause as much heartache as carrying around anger and resentment everywhere. Two victims suffer; the one who is not forgiven, and the one who will not forgive. When you refuse to forgive others, seeds of bitterness are planted in your own life. Over time the seeds grow into a pessimistic outlook on life itself. Happiness escapes your grasp. Only bad feelings and resentment remain. You can't go forward in life because you're chained to the past. But forgiveness frees you up to get on with life. Forgiveness shows strength in your character. Forgiveness shows mercy. Forgiveness demonstrates love to that other person. These are all qualities to be greatly desired. Forgiveness was modeled for us by God Himself as He forgave us our sins.

When you forgive someone who has wronged you, you gain a friend. That's why the Scriptures say, "We love God because He first loved us." And forgiving even the worst offender becomes easier when you consider just how much you have been forgiven by God.

God Can Use You in Your Weakness

"But he said to me, "My grace is sufficient for you, for my power is made perfect in weakness." Therefore I will boast all the more gladly about my weaknesses, so that Christ's power may rest on me."

2 Corinthians 12:9 NIV

There are times in life when unexpected things happen to us. A medical problem arises that is going to greatly restrict your life, or some other limitation has surrounded you and derailed your plans. For the believer, these setbacks not only affect the physical aspects of life but the spiritual ones as well. You begin to wonder, "How can I do what God was calling me to do now?". "How can I have any impact in ministry now? It looks like I have to spend all my time just trying to make it through the week." The thing to remember is that God has known every detail of your life from the beginning of time. When He designed a plan tailored specifically for you, He knew this day would come. And He knew the limitations you would have. So He also adjusted your ministry to accommodate your abilities. For example, if you can no longer travel, He will bring others to you. God made the universe from nothing. He can do wonderful things, even in your weakness.

God will be Your Defender

He only is my rock and my salvation; He is my defense;

I shall not be moved.

Psalm 62:6 NKJV

We all have times when someone says something about us that's meant to hurt us. Their motives may be personal, political, envy, or some other reason. They try to damage your reputation or make you feel bad. But it's important to remember to take the high road and to pray for them. Still, that may not always stop their hostilities. But consider this ... when you spend the time to defend yourself, it takes your attention off the things that God has called you to. For that reason, some of the attacks may even be spiritual in nature. The enemies of God will do whatever they can, through whoever is willing, to keep you from the work God has given you. You defeat these attacks by keeping your eye on the ball and continuing God's work. During his presidency, Abraham Lincoln once said, *"If I were to try to read, much less answer all the attacks made on me, this office might as well be closed for any other business."* Don't let the attacks that come against you take you off course. Let God take care of your defense.

Look Forward to Your Next Chapter in Life

"Your eyes saw my substance, being yet unformed. And in Your book they all were written, the days fashioned for me, when as yet there were none of them."

Psalm 139:16 NKJV

As can be seen in the verse above, God wrote the days of your life in His book before any of them existed. He knew from the beginning what decisions you would make and what path you would choose each day of your life. Then He designed a plan especially for you and threaded it like a beautiful tapestry through your story. Like any book, there are chapters in which you, the main character, experience different situations. There are the beautiful mountaintops where all is well, and there are the valleys below where trials act as fertile soil in which you grow. When life changes, don't be thinking your story is over, and God will not be using you any longer. No, He's just taking you into the next chapter. God is interested in using you every day of your life. And He has already made the necessary changes to accommodate the new conditions in the coming chapters. The Divine Author is penning a beautiful story using your days. Just wait until you see what He will do, in the next chapter of life!

Remember Where You're From and Why You're Here

"You are the light of the world. A city that is set on a hill cannot be hidden. Nor do they light a lamp and put it under a basket, but on a lampstand, and it gives light to all who are in the house. Let your light so shine before men, that they may see your good works and glorify your Father in heaven

Matthew 5:14-16 NKJV

Living life in the world makes it difficult for believers to remember that they are not of the world. But as the world becomes a darker place, believers begin to feel uncomfortable with the downward spiral of society. Things formerly considered bad are now considered good. Meanwhile good is treated as bad. Lawlessness is tolerated, and the love of many has grown cold. Marriage, formerly a beautiful act of love, is now shunned and derided by many. Perversion of every sort is an object of pride and claimed to be from "open minds". The world teaches that man is evolving. But the facts show that he is devolving. Yes, knowledge is increasing, but wisdom has exited the building. In this darkened environment, the light of Christ in your life must be allowed to shine and show to others, who seek the truth, the way back to God.

THE END

"Let the words of my mouth and the meditation of my heart be acceptable in Your sight, Oh Lord, my strength and my Redeemer."

Psalm 19:14 NKJV

ABOUT THE AUTHOR

Stephen Apple is an author who seeks to encourage the weary travelers among us. He has spoken to tens of thousands of people through the years, encouraging them to trust God with life and rest in His care.

STEPHEN APPLE

Made in the USA
Charleston, SC
28 December 2016